Advanced Fly Tying

Books by A. K. Best

Production Fly Tying
Dyeing and Bleaching Natural Fly-Tying Materials
A. K.'s Fly Box
Advanced Fly Tying

Advanced Fly Tying

The Proven Methods of a
Master Professional Fly Tyer

A. K. Best

Introduction by John Gierach

THE LYONS PRESS

Guilford, Connecticut
An imprint of The Globe Pequot Press

To John Gierach

There comes a time in everyone's life when it becomes necessary to admit who helped the most to get you where you are today. Thanks, John.

The Lyons Press is an imprint of The Globe Pequot Press.

Some of the material in this book has been previously published in some form on the pages of the following magzines and Web sites:

Fly Rod & Reel
Flyfishing and Tying Journal
Mid-Atlantic Fly Fishing Guide
Fly Rod & Reel Online (http://www.flyrodreel.com)
Virtual Fly Shop (http://www.flyshop.com)
Flyfishing Broadcast Network (http://www.fbn-flyfish.com)

Printed in China

10 9 8 7 6 5 4 3 2

The Library of Congress Cataloging-in-Publication Data is available on file.

Contents

———————— ✳

Preface

———————————— ✳

I was a musician for many years, and I discovered long ago that fly tying and fly fishing are much like studying music: The more you learn, the more you know you need to learn. It's a daily quest for unobtainable perfection. That thought shouldn't discourage anyone from either pursuit, since it's the journey, not the destination, that's so much fun.

Just as no two musicians will perform the same composition in an identical manner, fly tyers will use different techniques for tying the same fly pattern. What follows is my interpretation of how to apply some advanced techniques when tying trout flies. There are some new patterns as well as variations on some old standard patterns that have proven to be very effective during the past five to eight years of testing.

—A. K. BEST
BOULDER, COLORADO
SEPTEMBER 2001

Introduction

———————————————————————— ✳

A. K. has always been a detail man. You can see it in his camp kitchen (a slot for everything, everything in its slot), you can see it in his hand-tied leaders (he's the first fisherman I knew who owned a micrometer for measuring monofilament), and you can certainly see it in his flies.

You can also see it in his heightened sense of punctuality. If you're supposed to meet him at six in the morning to go fishing and you arrive fifteen minutes early, he'll already be standing out on the sidewalk next to his gear, waiting for you. At ten minutes till six, he'll start pacing. Once, years ago, we were supposed to take a guy fishing, but A. K. left without him because he was three minutes late, so he obviously wasn't coming.

As a fly tyer, A. K. is as meticulous and relentless as you'd expect, and as near as I can tell he doesn't do anything without a well-thought-out reason. In a way, that's what this book is about: how carefully you have to think about what you're doing if you want to become a top-notch fly tyer.

The best lesson I learned from A. K. over the years was just that: to think about what I was doing and, in the same vein, to question everything I heard and read, or at least stop short of believing it without question. As Kurt Andersen once said in a different context, you must always ask yourself, "What do I think I know, and why do I think I know it?"

I mean, yes, you should try to use the best dry-fly hackle you can get your hands on, but is there a point where it gets too good and therefore doesn't work as well? And yes, you should tie well-proportioned flies, but are the accepted proportions true to life, or are they arbitrary? This would include provisionally disregarding the common wisdom about flies and fly tying and returning to the source now and then for a fresh look.

Some time ago A. K. started tying short wing tips sticking out of the aft end of his beetle patterns, and that was uncharacteristic because he's much more likely to remove body parts from a pattern to make it quicker and easier to tie than he is to add something.

But of course his explanation makes sense. The first thing a beetle does before it flies is to open its shell slightly and extend the tips of its wings. A beetle that is floating in a trout stream doesn't want to be floating in a trout stream, so, even though he's not able to take off, he's probably made that first move and now he's stuck there like that, with just the tips of his wings sticking out.

A. K. didn't arrive at this through logic—the logic came later—he arrived at it by watching beetles taking off and others floating in streams. Really. I've fished with the guy for a long time now, and he really does go off by himself to do things like that. Do those little wing tips on beetle patterns make a difference? I'd have to say that nine times out of ten they don't, but then that tenth time—with a big, smart trout feeding in skinny water—they do.

That's how A. K. thinks. What he often ends up with is a fly that's entirely recognizable and still fairly easy to tie, but that is ever so slightly better: a pattern that may, in the right hands, fool a few more trout.

Some of the things in this book are agonizingly detailed: twenty-eight steps for saving time; an entire chapter on how to hold your hand while tying; and so on. It all seems to make sense, if not when you read it, then at least when you sit down at the vise to try it.

A. K.'s tying instructions come from long experience as a professional fly tyer, a job where time really is money, but that's not all of it. Plenty of people are very good at something, but few are so acutely aware of what they're doing, how they do it and why, and almost none are able to explain it clearly. A. K. is among the best fly tyers I've ever seen, and he is the best instructor.

When we first started fishing together, I was the sloppy one—always fumbling, always forgetting something, even late now and then, God help me. I've learned some things about organization and attention to detail from A. K.—both on the river and at the vise—and by now I'm a better fisherman and fly tyer because of his influence. But I guess by comparison I'm still the sloppy one. For instance, his tying bench looks like an operating room table before the operation, while mine looks like the spot where a raccoon recently killed a chicken.

Which is to say, you don't have to become a perfectionist yourself to learn from one.

—JOHN GIERACH
LYONS, COLORADO
AUGUST 2001

Advanced Fly Tying

ONE

Vise and Tool Care

✳

Many fly-tying books contain good information about the tools you'll need to tie flies. Based on that information and possibly some sage advice from your fly-tying friends and the folks at your local fly shop, you've probably purchased the tools your budget will allow. Whatever the quality and number of tools you have, I think it's important to know how to care for your investment if you expect your tools to function properly for many years to come.

VISE CARE

You should clean and lubricate your vise at least once a year. Most high-quality vises are packaged with instructions on cleaning and lubricating the moving parts. *Read and follow the manufacturer's instructions to the letter!* If you inadvertently threw away or lost this crucial document, contact the manufacturer for a new one, or you can follow the outline below.

First, assemble the following list of things you will need to clean and lube your vise:

1. Hand towel (you'll lay out all small parts on it to prevent loss).
2. Can of "canned air."
3. Two ½-by-12-inch strips of an old T-shirt.
4. Two 4-by-4-inch squares of an old T-shirt.
5. Keep the rest of the old T-shirt close at hand.
6. Allen wrenches if necessary.
7. Small tube of rubber cement. (Touch the tip of your Allen wrench to the rubber cement before inserting it into the Allen screw; it'll prevent the tiny Allen screws from jumping off and disappearing. The tiny amount of rubber cement left in the hole can easily be removed with an old needle.) It's also a good idea to apply the tiniest amount of rubber cement to one side of the threads on these tiny Allen screws before you put them back. This prevents them from working loose and falling out later.
8. Small pair of pliers. Use a 4-by-4-inch patch of T-shirt in the jaws to avoid marring vise parts.
9. Tweezers.
10. Small screwdriver set for slotted screws, if necessary.
11. Old toothbrush.
12. Pipe cleaners.
13. Small can of 3-in-1 oil and Gehrke's Gink.
14. Strip of triple-O emery cloth.
15. Can of lacquer thinner to cut and dissolve grease buildup.

Put a *few* drops of 3-in-1 oil on one of the ½-by-12-inch strips and one of the 4-by-4-inch squares of old T-shirt and put both in a small Ziploc bag the night before you disassemble your vise. The overnight rest will allow the oil to permeate the cloth pieces.

1. Lay out the hand towel and, if possible, remove the vise head from the standard or the collar.
2. Clean any screws removed with a toothbrush and clean the holes they were in with a pipe cleaner.

3. Blow the lint out of the threaded holes with the canned air and apply a thin film of oil to both the screws and the holes they were in.

4. Remove the collet and jaw assembly from the collar. Carefully clean the inside surface of the collar and the area of the collet that contacts it. Be on the lookout for thin metal or delrin washers, and wipe them clean. Buff all contacting surfaces with pieces of T-shirt until they are mirror smooth. Blow all the lint out of the collar with canned air and apply a thin film of oil with one of the oiled four-by-four-inch patches. (Or use Gehrke's Gink—it's a wonderful lubricant.)

5. Remove the cam lever pin and clean both the pin and the hole it was in. Inspect both the pin and the hole in the cam lever for excessive wear, and order new parts if necessary. Blow the lint from the hole with canned air, and apply a thin film of oil or Gink.

6. Inspect the cam surfaces for grooves or tracks. If there are tiny scratchlike marks, you may be able to buff them out with a piece of very fine emery cloth. Be very careful when doing this not to create any flat spots on the curved shoulders of the cam. If this area is distinctly grooved, you'd be wise to order a replacement part.

7. There is usually an adjustment nut that contacts the shoulders of the cam. Inspect it for indentations. If they're minor, you may be able to smooth them with the emery cloth. If they're deep and very distinct, order a new part.

8. Remove the jaws from the collet tube and inspect the inside shoulder of the end of the collet for wear and grit where the rear shoulder of the jaws contact. Buff both the collet tube opening and the jaw shoulders mirror smooth.

9. If you can't remove the jaws from the collet tube, adjust the jaws to their widest opening and clean with the oiled ½-by-12-inch strip of T-shirt by buffing between the collet opening and the rear shoulder of the jaws.

10. The cam pin, the cam surfaces, and the jaw shoulder/collet opening are the three areas of your vise that undergo the greatest amount of stress, friction, and wear. The cam pin may be

lubricated, since it's concealed in a hole. The cam surfaces, however—which are exposed—should never be oiled or greased! Both substances collect dust and will only increase the wear factor on these surfaces. The same is true for the collet opening and the rear shoulder of the jaws. Natural facial oils are the best. Regular cleaning of these three areas will add years to the life expectancy of your vise.

11. Tying with moist or damp materials or wet fingers can cause rust to appear. Carefully inspect your vise for any hints of rust, and buff it away immediately. A thin film of oil will help prevent rust from attacking your vise.

12. Mushrooming of the outside edges of the jaw opening—where it contacts the hook—can be repaired by smoothing down the edges with a very fine file or diamond dust hook hone. This will tend to slow the degeneration a bit. High-quality jaws are made of a material that's harder than the hook, but this isn't always so on the less expensive vises. If your jaws are replaceable, it's probably a good idea to order a new set.

13. You can restore and/or reshape the tips of your jaws if they're chipped on one or both sides by carefully filing away the tips until the chipped area is gone. Close the jaws, use a very fine flat file, and then remove the file tracks with a diamond dust hook hone. Cover the junction of the end of the collet tube and the rear shoulder of the jaws with masking tape to prevent tiny metal particles from dropping in. Don't try to hurry this repair. When you have finished, use the canned air to blow away any metal particles that may have accumulated between the jaws. Think of it as customizing your jaws: Some vises have jaws that are too thin at their tips. Never place a hook at the very tip edge of the jaws. Even a tiny hook placed too close to the edge can cause the jaw material to chip away.

Hints on vise use: *Apply only enough pressure to keep the hook from sliding up and down with the tying thread you're using!* Never try to make pretzels from your heavy hooks to demonstrate how well your vise holds a hook. It's a stupid thing to do, because if you're applying that much pressure on your hooks as you tie, you're probably fracturing every hook you put in the vise, you just ruined a perfectly good hook, and in any case, what kind of a fly are you going to tie with a hook that looks like that?

SCISSOR CARE AND SHARPENING

You should have at least two pairs of scissors: one for cutting threads and trimming fly-tying materials, and another that's a little heftier for cutting ribbing wire and heavy hair such as bucktail, elk, or deer body hair. These coarser materials will quickly dull the razor edge on the best scissors you can buy. It's a good idea to cut all wire materials as close to the blade axis as possible, because there's more cutting leverage there, and you'll preserve the tips of the blades for finer work.

Purchase a fine diamond dust hook hone made by Easy Lap, if you're brave enough to try to sharpen your scissor blades yourself. The honing section is flat on one side and round on the other, is about one-eighth inch wide, and fits into a cap much like a ballpoint pen. If you don't want to chance it, take your scissors to someone who sharpens scissors professionally—or buy a new pair.

Take a close look at the cutting edge of your scissor blades to determine the angle of the bevel on the cutting edges. Carefully stroke this beveled edge with the flat side of the hook hone with a downward motion toward the blade tip two or three times on each blade. Test the sharpness of your scissors by snipping off the tips of the fine marabou tufts at the base of a hackle feather. You have sharp scissors if your scissors will cleanly cut away the last one-sixteenth inch of this wispy material.

Improper storage can lead to damaged scissor blades. I strongly recommend that you find a small block of 2-by-4 lumber and drill some one-quarter-inch-diameter holes in one side that are 1½ inches deep and about 2 inches apart. Simply drop your scissor points into the holes for easy safe storage and quick access. Never toss your scissors into a drawer with other tools—the blades will be damaged.

DUBBING NEEDLES

Most tyers buy their dubbing needles. Avoid the kind that have heavy brass handles of small diameters. They're top heavy and difficult to pick up. I make my own dubbing needles by poking a darning needle into a 3- or 4-inch length of one-quarter-inch-square balsa wood. You can also make something that's a little more pleasing to the eye by drilling a small hole into a small piece of a bamboo rod's mid- or butt section and inserting the butt of a darning needle into it. A tiny drop of superglue will hold the needle in place forever. Magnetize the needle by stroking it over a strong magnet several times so you can use it to pick up tiny hooks. I store mine in the same 2-by-4 block with my scissors.

2 x 4 with scissors, dubbing needle, and dubbing teaser

DUBBING TEASERS

I've tried bore brushes, Velcro strips, and an assortment of other dubbing teaser ideas, but I still prefer the teaser made from a dentist's root canal tool. It looks like a fine length of stiff stainless-steel wire with several dozen barbs around it that point toward the butt end, which is usually mounted into a lightweight handle. It's the most effective and controllable dubbing teaser I've found. I advise making a cap that you can slide over the working end to protect it if none came with it. A malted milk straw works for most of them. Simply slide the straw over the teaser end and partially onto the handle. Cut it to a length about one-quarter inch longer than the barbed end. Always use the teaser *before* you apply head lacquer to the head of the fly to avoid getting any of the lacquer on the barbed portion of the teaser. Head lacquer is almost impossible to remove once it's there. You can remove natural oils and dubbing wax by soaking it in a small vial of head lacquer for a few minutes, then brushing the barbed portion with an old toothbrush. It's important to keep your metal teaser as clean as possible to prevent rust from forming.

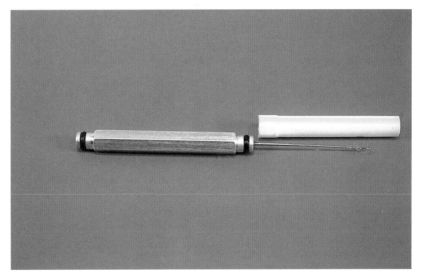

Dubbing teaser with straw cap

HAIR STACKERS

Choose a hair stacker with the least amount of wobble between the tube and the receiver. Check to be certain that the bottom is absolutely flat, with no rounded corners. Be sure that the stacked hair will protrude from the end of the tube far enough to be easily grasped. Avoid hair stackers with wide flared funnels. Long hair will get hung up on the wide rim, and it will take much longer to stack any kind of hair. Keep the outside and bottom of the tube and the inside of the receiver clean. It's surprising how rapidly natural oils from the various hairs used in a stacker can build up and collect dust, which can inhibit the stacker from functioning well. Simply buff the outside of the tube with an old T-shirt, then twist a portion of the shirt into the receiver.

HACKLE PLIERS

The best advice I can give you about the care of hackle pliers is this: When you find a pair that you believe is absolutely essential to your ability to tie flies, buy a backup pair immediately! Chances of losing the pair you have increase exponentially according to how much you believe you cannot get along without them.

TWO

Using Rotary Vises

✳

My definition of a rotary vise is one whose collet and jaw assembly can be turned 360 degrees repeatedly. Some tyers say that a vise is not a true rotary if the hook shank goes around in a little loop as the vise collet/jaw assembly is rotated. A true rotary vise is also often called an "in-line" rotary vise, since the hook shank rotates like an axle. I maintain that if something goes around and around, it's rotating.

I tied thousands of freshwater and saltwater flies on one of the first premium-quality rotary vises that Bill Hunter made, called the HMH. It was the seventy-ninth vise in a limited production of three hundred. I simply put the hook in the jaws upside down if I wanted the hook shank to be in line. I soon learned to allow my materials hand to flow back and forth with the looping hook shank. I got so good at it that the first time I tried to tie on one of the new in-line rotary vises, I couldn't do it! I have learned since, and must admit that all of the true rotary or in-line rotary vises I have tried basically do what their makers say. The hook shank goes around and around, and the hook shank stays in the center of the rotation. Your choice of a vise is entirely a matter of personal preference, which I'll address later.

The greatest value of a rotary vise is for the tyer who ties mostly large flies such as Woolly Worms, Woolly Buggers, long-shank streamers, Deceivers, and tarpon flies—any fly whose body material, ribbing, or palmered hackle requires many turns of firmly wrapped and evenly spaced material. Tying these with a rotary vise not only speeds up your tying but saves valuable material as well, because you can tie in the end of whatever is on a spool or skein, wrap it forward using the rotary function of the vise, and clip it off when you're finished. You can forget all about that direction in a fly recipe that says "cut off an 8-inch piece of tinsel." The only waste will be the last 2 or 3 inches on the spool.

The material you apply to the hook shank will be tied on much tighter and with a greater degree of control. The bodies will be smoother, and the ribbing more evenly spaced. I've only seen three or four tyers use the rotary feature of a vise to wind on the hackle collar on a dry fly. I've tried it, but I didn't feel comfortable with it since my method of hackling dry flies is unconventional.

Another equally valuable use is being able to give the jaws a slight twist to either side to check the symmetry of wing sets on dry flies, wrapping the bases of split hairwings and parachute wing posts, tying in split goose biot tails on stonefly nymphs, or checking to see if the wing case on a nymph is set squarely on top of the hook.

As if these weren't enough reasons to jump up right now and go to your nearest fly shop to buy a new vise, here's some more neat stuff you can do with a rotary vise:

1. You no longer have to remove a hook from the vise and invert it, as directed in some instructions; simply rotate the jaw assembly 180 degrees and the hook will be upside down or inverted.
2. Give the jaws a twist to expose the belly or thorax of your nymphs before you use the dubbing teaser.
3. Trimming a spun deer-hair head on Muddlers and bass bugs is much easier. Near-perfect symmetry can be achieved with either scissors or a razor blade.

4. You can guide a small drop of head lacquer completely around the head of the tiniest dry fly or nymph by simply rotating the head.

5. Paint epoxy or head lacquer on the long noses of tarpon flies while rotating the head assembly. This will ensure even and complete coverage of either product.

6. Use the vise as an epoxy dryer by slowly rotating the hook while the epoxy sets to prevent sagging.

7. Apply self-adhesive eyes, or paint eyes with eye sticks.

8. Wrapping wire-bound dubbing brushes or thread-bound dubbing loops while rotating the head will absolutely prevent any gaps or overlaps.

9. Palmer hackling with two or even three feathers at a time can easily be accomplished.

Browse through your favorite fly-fishing or fly-tying magazine for advertisements of rotary vises. Study the design of each one carefully. Go to your nearest fly shop and play with the models on display. Be as critical about the various features as you can. The vise you purchase should hold all the hook sizes and styles *you* use firmly with a minimum of adjustment. You're not going to be making pretzels with your hooks, but the jaws should always hold a hook firmly enough that your heaviest thread will break before the hook slips up or down.

Be extremely cautious about the jaw closure devices. Some cam levers can pinch your thumb or finger as you close the jaws. Some have knurled knob jaw-closing devices. If these knobs are too small, you'll rip the pads of your thumb and forefinger after a dozen or so flies. If these knobs are too big, you'll be constantly snagging material on them. The outside surfaces of the entire jaw assembly and the housing for the rotating arm should be as clean as possible. Is the in-line adjustment for different hook sizes easy to accomplish? No tools should be required for simple, daily use of your vise.

Be certain that the crook or bent arm is large or deep enough to accept the heel of your hand. This is a shortcoming on some bent-arm vises I've seen. Finally, look for a simple device that will lock out the rotary function when you don't need it.

THREE

Saving Time

———————————— ✳

I'm often asked, "How fast can you tie a dozen flies?" Or, "How many flies can you tie in an hour?" I usually answer with, "It depends on the pattern and how well my head is connected to my fingers that day." As you probably know, some saltwater patterns take as long as fifteen or twenty minutes each to tie well. Then again, some midge larvae can be tied in as little as ninety seconds. But whenever I'm asked these questions, I always admonish the person asking to not worry about it! Commercial tyers should determine how many flies they can comfortably tie in a week, leaving out at least one day for fishing. I determine how much money I need to make in the week ahead, and when I arrive at that amount, I go fishing! If you tie for speed, your flies will soon begin to show your haste. Every tyer will develop what I call a cruising speed—whether you're a rank amateur about to tie six #14 Adams or an experienced pro about to tie six dozen #14 Adams. Both tyers will settle into a groove that will result in a consistently well-tied fly. If either tyer attempts to rush in order to increase output, he will suffer poorly tied flies.

Having said all that, there are a lot of things that both the amateur and the pro can do to *save time*. Saving time is the key to increasing your output and tying better-looking, more durable flies. It's not tying any faster, it's saving time between steps 1, 2, and 3 while you tie. The way to save time is to eliminate unnecessary hand movements with tools and materials.

The following are some of the things I do every day to save time, increase my output, and tie consistently durable flies, without rushing to complete them.

1. *Learn to keep your scissors in your hand!* Every time you lay them down you'll have to pick them up again, which wastes time and breaks your rhythm.
2. *Learn to whip-finish by hand!* Once again, you'll save a second or two if you don't have to look for yet another tool, pick it up, and put it back when finished. And you'll be able to tie off a much cleaner, tighter head with more thread placement control.
3. Lay out all the materials you'll need to tie two flies or two dozen flies of the same pattern and size, including counting out the hooks. This means pulling and sizing the hackle, tailing, and wings as well as laying out the body materials. Place these materials in close proximity to the vise, because that's where your hands spend most of their time. I place hooks, hackles, and tailing to the right side of my vise and body and winging materials to the left. You can save an enormous amount of time if you purchase a couple of small-parts cabinets. My favorite has thirty drawers: six drawers in each column, five columns across. I put different-colored spade hackles for tailing in the bottom drawer of each column, then work my way up in hackle size: #20, 18, 16, 14, and, at the top, #12. Label each column of drawers with the color of the hackle and each drawer with the size. You can pluck and size

the hackle from half a dozen necks in just a couple of hours. Then, next time you want to tie some flies, all you have to do is pull out the drawer with the size hackle you want, count out the hackles needed, and set out the tailing drawer; now all you need is winging and body material. It sure beats having to pick up the dry-fly neck and find the right-sized hackle for each fly! Another advantage to pulling hackle ahead of time is that you will be able to select hackles for length as well. This will allow you to get the same number of hackle turns on each fly. Lay out sized winging material as well.

Parts cabinet, materials laid out, spooled bobbins, stacked dubbing containers, scissors, and dubbing teaser

4. If you use the standard loop scissors, hone all the outside surfaces round and smooth so that you can insert the closed points into the final loop of a hand whip-finish as you pull it tight. It'll save you time in not having to pick up your bodkin and put it back for the same purpose.

Loop scissors in whip-finish loop

5. Magnetize your bodkin and needlenose pliers. This will make
    picking up tiny hooks a breeze!

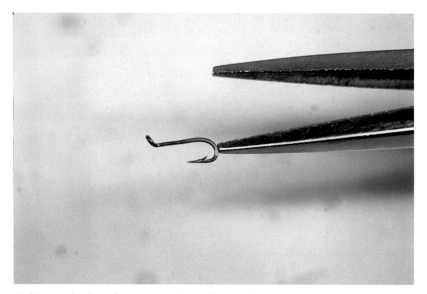

Picking up hook with magnetized needlenose pliers

6. Keep several bobbins spooled with the colors and thread sizes you use most often. It saves the time it takes to spool a bobbin with new thread each time you tie a new pattern. (See photo on page 15.)

7. Learn to use a bobbin cradle to keep the bobbin from hanging down in the exact spot where you don't want it when you're wrapping a quill or, worse yet, while you're hackling a dry fly. By having the bobbin well out of the way, you'll be able to focus your attention on a single act rather than two at once. I don't like the bobbin cradles that are attached to the upright stem of the vise, because the thread length changes each time I rotate the arm of the cradle. I prefer a freestanding bobbin cradle that attaches to the bench with its own C-clamp. If you can't find one or don't want to spend the time making your own, a plastic iced tea glass with some weight in the bottom works quite well.

8. Find or build a work surface of the proper height to prevent backaches and neck aches. Almost all tables and desks are too high for use as a fly-tying bench. You must remember that your vise has an upright stem that places your work area at least 6 inches higher than the desktop. The orthopedic secret here is to keep your forearms as close to horizontal as possible—15 to 20 degrees is acceptable. I built my own fly-tying bench years ago with a work surface that's only 28 inches from the floor. The top is light almond-colored formica with an eggshell finish. It's a soft color that doesn't reflect glaring light.

9. Get a good, comfortable office chair, one that has adjustments for both seat height (I raised mine as high as it would go and haven't had a back- or neck ache in years) and backrest placement. The only part of your body that should ache after a few hours at the vise is your butt.

10. Use good light! I have a bank of fluorescent tubes in the ceiling over my bench and a 100-watt bulb in my tying lamp, which is only 6 inches above my vise head. The incandescent bulb eliminates the "buzz effect" of fluorescent tubes, which causes eyestrain and headaches for some tyers.

11. If you're going to tie a lot of tiny flies—say, #20 and smaller—either go see your optometrist for a pair of glasses that will focus at 10 or 12 inches or go to the drugstore and get a pair of magnifiers.

12. Store your dubbing blends in stackable round plastic containers that are large enough to attach a label indicating both the color and type of dubbing. Place another label on the back side of each container with the recipe you used to create each shade of dubbing in each container. (See photo on page 15.)

13. Keep all your dry-fly necks, bucktails, squirrel tails, hen necks, turkey and goose quills, dyed quills, peacock eyes—anything that's long and could get bent out of shape—in long plastic sleeves.

14. Store all of the items in hint 13, above, in plastic shoeboxes that you can label with the contents.

15. If you use dubbing wax, remove it from the round tube it came in, melt it, and pour it into a flat container with a removable lid that you can attach to your bench with a little dab of florist's putty. Such a container will allow you to merely stroke the surface of the wax with your forefinger once or twice, and you're ready to dub. In most instances, dubbing wax belongs on your thumb and forefinger; this will give you greater control over the material you're trying to attach to the thread.

16. Keep your tying bench clean. When you're finished tying a pattern, put everything away.

17. Set goals! "Tonight I'm going to tie six #18 Adams" or, "Today I'm going to tie ten dozen #18 Adams." Stay at it until you've accomplished the goal. Then quit! If you're a commercial tyer, take a five-minute break every hour. It'll help keep you fresh.

18. Spray all your turkey, goose, and duck quills with Krylon Workable Fixatif. It's a clear spray that dries quickly and holds the individual fibers of a quill segment together while you tie it onto the hook.

19. Use a cork and a hat pin for head lacquer application. This combination is infinitely adjustable—and, most important, it isn't top heavy.

20. Put a small dab of florist's putty on the bottom of your head lacquer bottle to prevent it from skating all over your work-

Hat pin in cork

bench—or worse yet, tipping over. You'll need only one hand to grasp the cork/hat pin applicator to apply one tiny drop of head lacquer to a #22 dry fly, since the florist's putty will hold the bottle firmly to your tying bench.

21. Keep the end of your bobbin tube close to the hook shank as you tie the fly. One inch of thread between the end of the bobbin tube and the hook is plenty. You'll gain greater material and thread placement control, and it's quicker to wrap a 1-inch length of thread around the hook than it is 3 or 4 inches.

22. Keep the bobbin in your hand after finishing a fly. If you put it down while you take the fly out of the vise and replace it with another hook, you'll only have to pick it up again. That's wasted motion and time.

23. Get a length of 2-by-4-inch lumber of a length appropriate for your bench and drill three-sixteenth-inch holes (not all the way through!) about 2 inches apart as a place to store spooled bobbins. Keep the bobbins you use most often in the center of your bench where they'll be within easy reach. (Again, see the photo on page 15.)

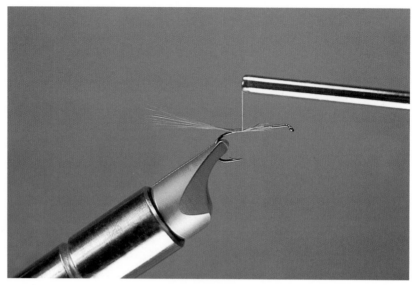

Short thread between bobbin tube and hook

24. Get a shorter piece of 2-by-4-inch lumber to store tools that you'll need on a daily basis, such as tweezers, needlenose pliers, bobbin threader, heavy scissors, Allen wrenches, and so on. Drill holes that best suit your needs. If you store these items in a drawer, you'll have to sort through the drawer each time you need one of them—additional wasted time. (See photo on page 15.)

25. Store seldom-used tools such as small pliers, wire side cutters, screwdrivers, and combs in an extra small-parts drawer.

26. An additional small-parts cabinet is a very convenient place to keep boxes of hooks you use most often. I put dry-fly hooks in a column of drawers, beginning with #24 and 26 in the same drawer at the bottom of the column, working my way up with #22 and 20 in the next drawer, then #18, 16, 14, and 12, each in its own drawer. I put nymph hooks in the next column, streamer hooks in the next, long-shank dry-fly hooks in the next, and miscellaneous hooks and sizes in the last column. Label each column with the hook manufacturer and style, then label each drawer with hook size. All your hooks are within short reach and easy to find.

27. Purchase the highest-quality tools and materials that your pocket will allow. Both will allow you to tie great-looking flies with increased efficiency. You simply cannot tie good-looking flies with inferior materials or tools.
28. Tie at least one fly every day.

In other words, get organized and think methodically.

All the above ideas will help you establish a rhythm to your tying, and rhythm is the key to consistency and production. Some of the ideas outlined above may seem a little awkward at first—but so did learning to tie your own shoes. I'll bet you can do it without thinking now.

Finally, you must remember that we all have good days when everything goes better than we expect. Enjoy them! Then there are those days when nothing seems to go right. Relax and struggle through it, because that will be your tying rate for the day. Or just tell yourself, "To hell with this, I'm going fishing!"

FOUR

Hand Position

———————————————— ✳ ————

It's been said that location is the key to success in many of our endeavors. When it comes to tying flies, hand position is the key. I'm talking about the position of your materials hand and how the materials are held in it. If you're a right-hander, it would be your left hand. Your right hand is the bobbin hand. But before I get into hand position in the following hints, I believe it's most important to get the angle of the vise collet set in the proper position. I've taught a lot of fly-tying classes in the past twenty years and often see tyers having trouble getting material tied onto the hook simply because they have the vise collet set at a horizontal position. This makes it nearly impossible for the materials hand to be placed in a position that will allow the tyer to wrap thread around almost anything.

Set the angle of the collet to a 45- to 50-degree angle. This angle will allow you to place your materials hand on the vise in a more normal position when you hold material against the hook. Normal hand position can be demonstrated if you stand up and allow your arms to hang down at your sides in a relaxed manner. Your thumbs will probably touch the outside seams of your trousers, and the palms of your hands face the outside of your thighs. Now raise your forearms to a horizontal position. Your palms probably face each other. When you swing both arms toward each other in a clapping motion, your palms will touch. If you do this a second time, you'll notice how little effort is required to rotate your palms to a 45-degree or even a palms-down position, yet it's almost painful to rotate your hands beyond horizontal or to a "thumbs-down" position, which is a nonresting hand position. You'll also notice that the rotation described above occurs at the elbow; if you rotate your hand to a thumbs-down position, you'll notice that your elbow will raise slightly and move away from your body, which causes discomfort after a short time. If you're tying with your materials hand in a thumbs-down position, your elbow will be raised and extended away from your body, which may cause aching neck muscles, a tired arm, and a sore elbow. Any hand position from palms vertical to palms horizontal can be considered normal hand position, with a 45-degree palm position being the most comfortable.

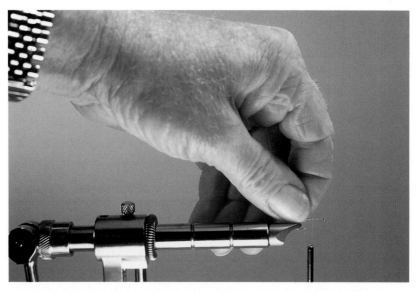

Vise at horizontal with materials hand. Notice unnatural hand position.

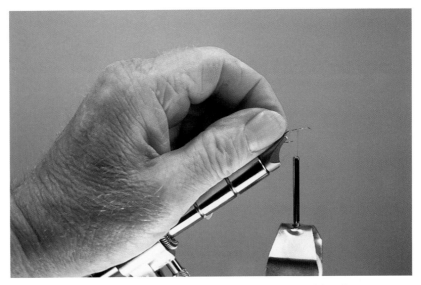

Vise at 45-degree angle with materials hand. Notice natural hand position

The most important thing to remember about hand position is that the material you're holding in your materials hand should be lined up in such a way that its centerline is at a 45-degree angle down from the centerline of your thumb. Imagine holding a toothpick (which would represent the material) between your thumb and forefinger. The toothpick should be at a 45-degree angle with the centerline of your thumb. The centerline of your forefinger will automatically be in line with the material. Holding materials in this manner automatically removes the first knuckle of your first finger from obstructing thread wraps over the top of the hook, since many materials must be held at a 45-degree angle to the hook shank before making the first wrap of thread.

A very common mistake made by tyers who are having trouble getting materials tied where they want them is that in nearly every instance, the material isn't touching the hook. It is essential that any material be touching the hook before you make the first wrap of thread to hold it in place. When thread touches material that's not in contact with the hook, the first thing it will do is move the material out of position. If the material is already touching the hook, the thread cannot move it. Holding materials as shown above will allow

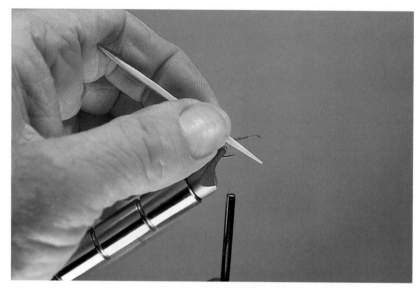

At the vise, with hook and thread attached, toothpick at 45-degree angle with centerline of thumb and in line with forefinger

you to place them against the hook before applying the first turn of thread. This position also keeps the first knuckle of your forefinger out of the way so that you can wrap the first turn of thread perpendicular to the hook. There should never be more than 1 inch of thread between the end of the bobbin tube and the hook shank. This will allow you to take one controlled, loose turn of thread over the material and place the thread over the material in exactly the right place. Quickly tighten the thread and allow thread torque to do its thing to twist the material into its final position.

The second most important thing to remember has to do with the pads on your thumb and forefinger. That's the area immediately beneath your thumbnail and first fingernail. It's the place where you hold the material as you place it on the hook. Take a moment and press your forefinger against your thumb as if you were holding something there. You'll see a rather prominent V-shaped area between the end of your forefinger and thumb. Roll them both toward their tips and watch the V-shaped area close to almost nothing. It should look somewhat like the little dent in the top of the letter *m*.

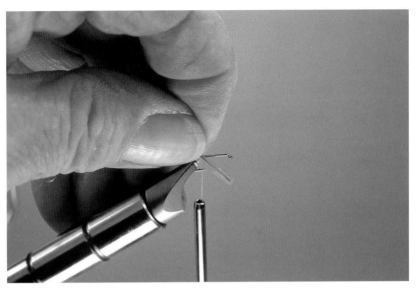

Incorrect alignment of materials and finger placement. Note how the knuckle of the forefinger gets in the way of making an exact placement of the first turn of thread.

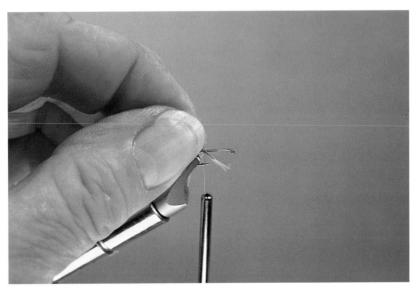

Correct alignment of materials and finger placement. Note that the knuckle of the forefinger is now out of the way.

This is the thumb and forefinger placement you should have while holding any material to be tied onto the hook.

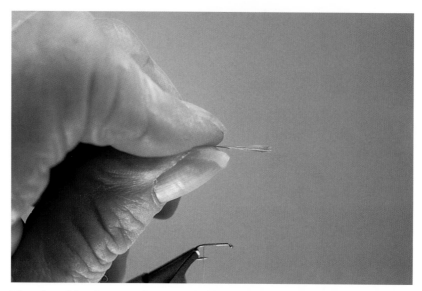

Thumb and forefinger with open V, holding toothpick. Notice how the open V space prevents proper placement of both the material and the thread.

When your thumb and forefinger are in this position, your thumbnail will become a thread guide as you make the first turn of thread around the material and the hook. The tying thread will slide off your thumbnail and onto the material, which is the most precise method possible to get material and thread onto the hook exactly where you want them, as shown in the lower photo on page 29.

Much of what I have just discussed isn't given a great deal of attention in the fly-tying books I own. If you carefully examine the step-by-step photos of how to tie certain fly patterns in your own books and many magazine articles, you'll see very few photos with the tyer's hand in the picture. The primary reason for that is the belief that no one wants to see a photo of someone's thumb. So the photos are often taken after the material has been tied in place. But the position of the tyer's thumb and forefinger and the way the material is held there is often the most important part of the photo. In

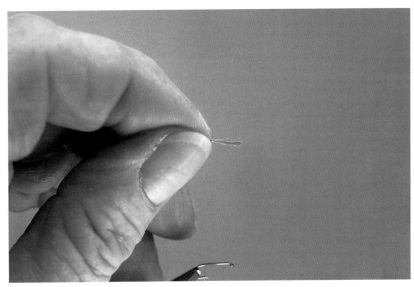

Thumb and forefinger rolled together like an m. *Note how the closed position allows proper placement of both material and thread.*

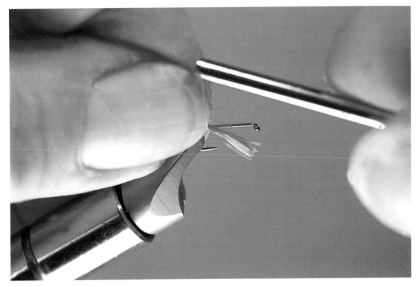

Thread sliding off thumbnail

addition, it isn't always easy to actually hold the materials as you would when tying as you take photos of this nature. The result is that many of us pick up habits that inhibit our ability to tie flies with ease. In other words, we are inadvertently being taught to do something that the author and photographer had no intention of teaching. We all know that it's much more difficult to unlearn a habit than it is to learn a new one. In the case of fly tying, it's essential to have proper hand position. It will make tying flies much more enjoyable. Your flies will not only look better but also last longer.

If you're thinking about purchasing a rotary vise with a bent arm, be sure that you'll have enough space for the heel of your hand in the little crook behind the jaws. If you're thinking of purchasing a new vise in a standard configuration, be sure that the angle of the jaws can be adjusted. Whichever type of vise you choose, whether rotary, standard, C-clamp, or pedestal, you'll save yourself a lot of aggravation (not to mention sore neck and back muscles) if you tie with an angle of about 45 degrees. Find or build a tying bench whose top is only about 28 inches from the floor, and get a chair that has both height and backrest adjustments. Adjust the seat height to the point where your forearms are as close to horizontal as possible. The chair should have no armrests. A soft cushion or two placed on the chair seat will often make your tying height much more comfortable in several respects.

The following photos demonstrate the proper hand position and materials placement between your thumb and forefinger for many of the common materials you will be applying to the hook.

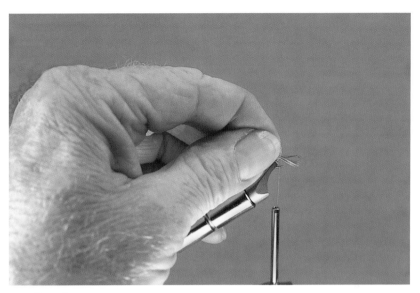

Dry-fly tailing

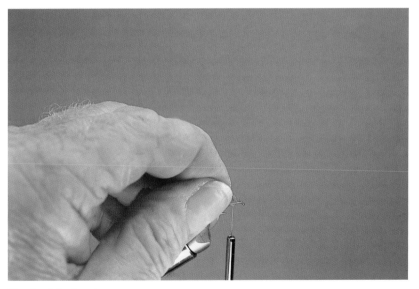

Hen hackle tip wings

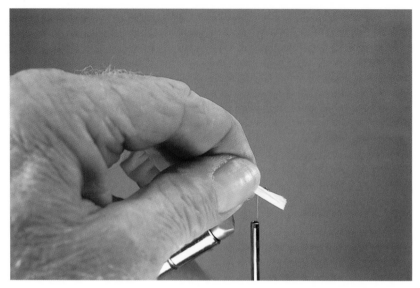

Parachute wing post and Wulff-style wings

Caddis hairwings

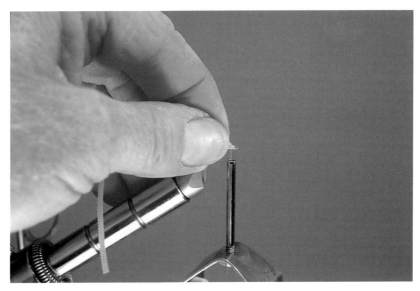

Midge wing strips

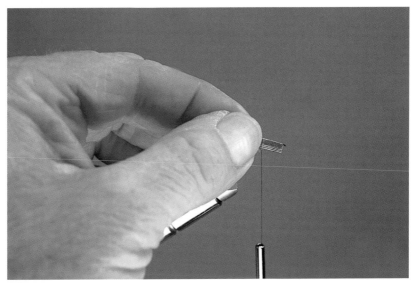

Quill-segment nymph wing pads

Woolly Bugger flash

Streamer hairwing

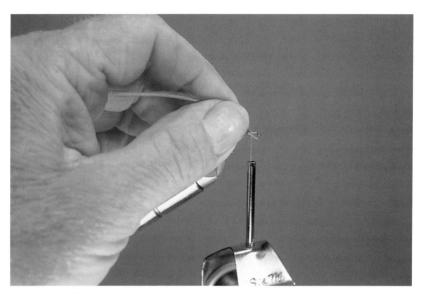

Dry-fly hackle

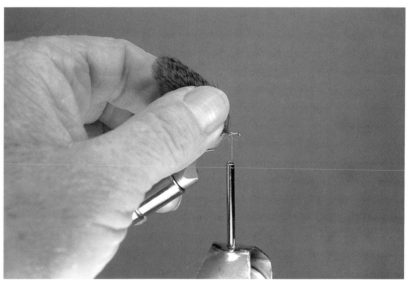

Wet-fly hackle

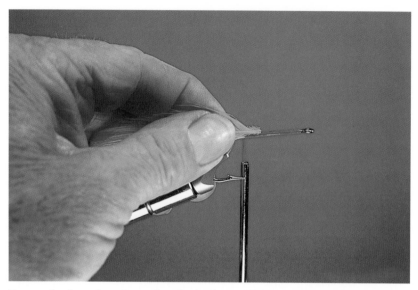

Tarpon feather wings. Note that the feather quills are in line with the center-line of the thumb.

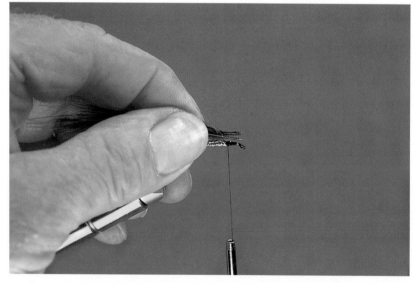

Freshwater streamer feather-type wings. Note that the feather quills are in line with the centerline of the thumb.

FIVE

Necks or Saddles?

＊

When I began tying flies commercially, I bought India rooster necks in lots of three hundred to five hundred for about a buck apiece. They were about all that was available at the time, they came in nearly all the colors I needed, I could dye the cream/white necks to several shades of dun, and they were cheap. The individual hackle fibers were pretty stiff, but the feathers were quite short. It was a rare neck that had #16 or 18 feathers that would allow me to take more than two turns of hackle. It was tedious work to tie five or six dozen #16 Hendricksons because it often took more time to find a dozen #16 hackles than it did to tie twelve flies. Size 18 and 20 dry flies were nearly impossible. There were quite a lot of tyers in those days who simply wrapped the hackle collar and then trimmed it to size, since it was a lot quicker and the trout didn't seem to mind. It's not unusual these days to hackle a dozen #16 flies with one and a half saddle hackle feathers! It still seems a little weird to lay out four feathers and be able to tie a dozen Adams.

Left to right: India neck, genetic neck, genetic saddle

The bulk India rooster necks I used to buy were ungraded. That is to say, they weren't marked #1, #2, or #3, as most necks are marked today. Fly tyers who bought these necks in bulk had to figure out their own system for grading them, mine being a couple of boxes labeled OKAY and BAD. A few people were raising roosters for fly tying in those days, but if you weren't already on their list, you were out of luck. Those of us who were just getting started had to make do with what was available. Most of the dry-fly hackle available to me was what I now call barnyard quality. And I, like lots of other tyers, even tried my hand at raising some birds of my own. It was not entirely successful.

Then along came Buck Metz, and the lives of just about every fly tyer in the country changed. There were a lot more smiling faces at the tying bench—and a lot more good-looking flies. Buck Metz made the most important contribution to fly tying in this century by making top-quality hackle available to the masses. Following closely behind in terms of production were Henry Hoffman and his famous grizzly necks, Bill Keough of Keough Hackles, and, lately, Dr. Tom Whiting of Whiting Farms. I don't want to leave anyone

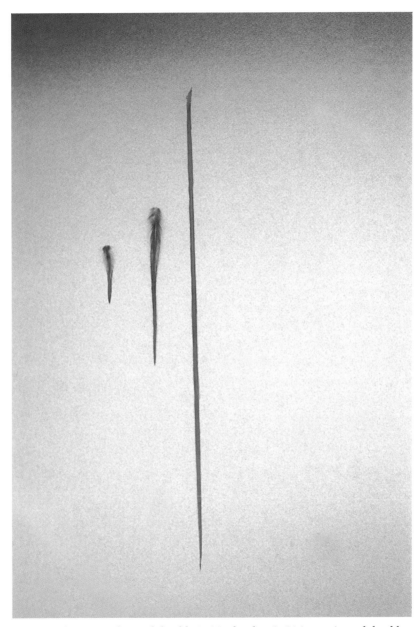

Left to right: #14 India neck hackle (1¼ inches long), #14 genetic neck hackle, #14 genetic saddle hackle

out of this chronology, but there are too many to list here. Take a look at the last issue of your favorite fly-tying or fly-fishing magazine and note the number of advertisements for hackle. Every hackle grower there is offering fine products. In my opinion, Buck Metz and Henry Hoffman were the leaders in what has become a revolution in hackle quality for the world.

Genetic control of the flocks and the occasional addition of new breeding stock have produced necks and saddles in recent years that are truly amazing. I've heard of one major hackle grower who is attempting to raise roosters with longer legs to keep the long saddle hackles from dragging on the floor! Where will it end?

It seems that saddle hackles are being pushed on us by every hackle grower in the country. They have beautiful products. The colors are getting better each year, and the length of the individual feathers is seldom shorter than 11 inches. Not only that, the hackle fiber count per inch is increasing, which means you can now fully hackle a dry fly with only three or four turns of saddle hackle—on a pattern that used to require six or seven turns of neck hackle. I remember having to use two neck hackles on some flies to get it right. And the ever-finer hackle quills are getting stronger.

Which to choose—necks or saddles? Or both? We've all known for a long time that we can invest large amounts of cash in a supply of necks or saddles. But which way should we go? How do we get the most for our dollars? Hopefully, some of the following will help you decide.

There are some problems with saddle hackle. The first problem is that there are usually no more than two or three different hackle sizes on any given saddle patch. The second and most frustrating problem is that the traditional grading of #1, #2, or #3 that has been used for years for neck hackle doesn't necessarily indicate the size of flies you'll be able to tie from a given saddle patch. The grading system for saddles seems to have more to do with the quality and length of the feathers than with their size. Nearly as frustrating is the fact that you'll often find a single saddle hackle feather to contain two (sometimes three) different hackle fiber lengths. When buying saddle patches you simply must use a hackle gauge to determine the size of the hackles. Those long, skinny, threadlike hackles that appear to be #20 and 18 are often #16 and 14. When you begin tying, you must use a hackle gauge for the entire length of each feather to avoid undersizing or oversizing the hackle collar. Considering the hundreds of necks and saddles that must be graded by someone who may not be a fly tyer, there will always be some margin of error, no matter what the source. Also, it isn't easy to find saddle patches for #12 and larger dry flies. I tie a lot of #12 Colorado Green Drakes with olive-dyed grizzly mixed with medium dun for the hackle collar. I have lots of #12 medium dun neck hackle left over from years of tying little Blue-Winged Olives, so that color isn't a problem. Grizzly is another matter, though. I once ordered two dozen #4 grizzly saddle patches and was assured they would contain mostly #12 and 10 hackles with a few #14. Of the two dozen saddle patches, only four had mostly #12 hackle. The remaining twenty saddles all contained #16 and 14 hackles with only a few #12.

I purchase all my tying supplies from wholesalers—with the exception of saddles, which I prefer to use when hackling parachute and fluttering caddis patterns. I go to one of the nearby fly shops with my hackle gauge, make my selections, and pay retail. I figure it's worth it in the long run, because I get exactly what I want in the shortest amount of time. Once I found a #3 brown saddle whose hackles were mostly #16 and 18 with a dozen or more #20.

So once again the fly tyer is faced with some agonizing choices. Saddles or necks? Saddles do have a much greater yield in terms of the number of dry flies that can be tied from one saddle. The neck, however, will allow you to tie many more different sizes of hackles, plus the spades for tailing, and the neck butt feathers for streamer wings and quill bodies. You'll have to purchase several necks to equal the yield from one saddle per hook size. But you'll also have to purchase three or four saddle patches to find all the hackle sizes you need on one neck. Add to this the fact that you're going to need the following minimum basic colors: grizzly, brown, medium dun, light dun, ginger, cream, and black. That's a total of seven necks to tie almost any dry fly from #22 through 10. To achieve the same size range with saddles would require a minimum of three saddle patches per color, or twenty-one saddles! However, if you consider the number of flies you can tie from twenty-one saddle patches, you'll probably spend more money for necks to tie the same number

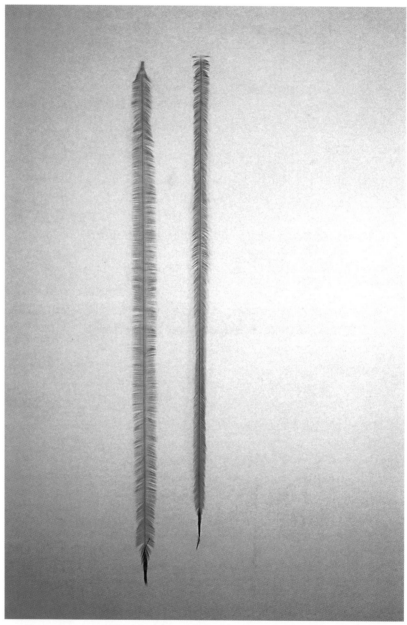

Saddle hackle showing different hackle fiber lengths. Note the exceptional evenness of the hackle fiber length on the saddle to the left, and the more typical variety of hackle fiber lengths on the hackle to the right.

of flies. You'll just be spending a little less a little more often. Cash flow can be a consideration.

Dry-fly neck retail prices range from as much as $125 to as little as $25, with an average cost being about $75 per neck. Saddles range from $90 to a low of $12, with an average cost of $51 per saddle. Generally speaking, you get about what you pay for. If you want the very best, you're going to have to pay for it. The more expensive necks will contain more feathers that are longer and come in a wider range of hackle sizes, often down to #24 and 26, with a few #28—and possibly some #32 for those tyers looking to tie a fly that looks like windblown chaff. The top-of-the-line saddles will have much longer hackle feathers and more of them, but you'll still be pretty much limited to two or three hook sizes per saddle with a dozen or so hackles on either side of that.

At first glance it looks like a no-brainer: Saddles are cheaper and you get a greater yield of flies per dollar, right? Take another look at it. Carefully decide what size of flies you tie the most and what your budget will allow; then make your purchases very selectively. Seven top-of-the-line dry-fly hackle necks (one of each color listed above) at $125 each will set you back $875. If we can agree that it will take three saddles to equal all the hook sizes available on one neck, then twenty-one top-of-the-line saddles will set you back a whopping $1,890! Using an average cost per neck of $75, seven medium-grade necks will cost you $525—compared to twenty-one medium-grade saddles at an average cost of $51 per patch, which will dent your wallet to the tune of $1,071! Think about where you're going to find #20 and smaller hackles before you go buy saddle or neck hackle.

What do I do? Except for grizzly, I order #3 cream/white necks and dye them. I am an admitted traditionalist in many respects. Some will go so far as to call me a bit stubborn, with a few other descriptive terms thrown in, but I still prefer neck hackle. My reasons are simple and traditional. I can get all the hackle sizes I need from a single neck, usually #22 through 12, and there is the very important bonus of spade hackles for tailing. I haven't been able to find them on any saddle in the lengths I need without stacking them. Large streamer and bass bug necks are now available from which you can find some usable tailing material, but it adds to the cost of producing dry flies. These days, individual neck hackles contain hackle fibers of a consistent length almost to the tip of each feather, and the hackle fiber count per inch is getting better as well. They are from the same bird as saddles, aren't they? I am almost assured of some web on each hackle feather when I order #3 necks, which I prefer because I can achieve the illusion of a thicker thorax area on the completed fly. When waterproofed with a silicone-based fly floatant, the softer web *doesn't soak up water.* And I can even use some of the stripped neck butt hackle feathers for quill bodies. The quills on saddles are simply too thin for this use.

I've traveled around the country a lot in the past twenty years or so conducting fly-tying classes and demonstrations. There are always a few people who hang around after each session to ask questions about some of the finer points of fly tying. One question comes up with what seems to be increasing frequency: "How can I prevent tippet twist?" I respond by asking a few questions of my own in an attempt to define an answer. "How long have you been tying?" "Do you false-cast a lot?" "What are you using for winging material?" "Are your wings perfectly set?" "Have you always had this problem?" (I start to sound like a therapist here.) "Does it happen with all your dry flies or just with upright-wing mayfly patterns?" "What kind of hackle are you using?" "How fine is your tippet?" "What size fly?"

The answer to the cause of tippet twist has been evading me, because the answers to my questions are usually: "I've been tying ten to twenty years." "I false-cast as little as possible." "It doesn't matter what winging material I use, it even happens when I use soft hen hackle tips for wings." "Yes, I set my wings perfectly to eliminate any propeller effect." "I never used to have a problem with tippet twist." "I use the best saddle hackle I can find." "Fly size doesn't seem to make a difference." "It even happens when I use 5X."

In a large number of instances I have seen the flies in question; they're beautifully tied, well-proportioned flies. Yet I personally have never had a problem with tippet twist with any of my dry flies, even when casting a #12 Green Drake on 6X. For a while I thought the answer might lie in the fact that tippet material is becoming limper with each passing year. I no longer believe that this is the case, because I was recently told by a fly tyer of twenty years' experience (whom I happen to know quite well) that he experiences tippet twist when casting a Bivisible! When I asked him what hackle he was using, he said, "The very best saddle hackle I can find." In nearly every instance of a fly tyer or fisher having problems with tippet twist, the choice of hackle has been top-grade saddle.

All this brings me to my current theory on the primary cause of tippet twist: The hackle stem is normally in the shape of an elongated oval, with shorter oval-shaped hackle fibers growing from each side of it. We traditionally wrap the hackle forward, putting a slight angle on each of the hundreds of oval-shaped hackle fibers, which creates what amounts to a miniature uncased turbine. If the hackle fibers are stiff enough, I believe this little turbine will rotate just enough to twist the hell out of your tippet.

I believe I haven't been experiencing tippet twist because I'm using lower-grade neck hackle that is slightly softer and has some web. These hackle fibers tend to bend back when the fly is cast. The hackling method I describe in *Production Tying* and *A. K.'s Fly Box*,

Traditionally wrapped saddle hackle (front view)

A. K.'s style of neck hackle (front view)

and which has also been explained in Leeson and Shollmeyer's *The Fly Tier's Benchside Reference* and Dave Hughes's *Trout Flies,* is intended to allow the hackle quill to twist. This will make the hackle fibers lean both backward and forward, which creates a bushier hackle collar and may also reduce the possibility of tippet twist.

I recently discussed much of this latest theory with George Harvey, who said "Yup, could be," and indicated that he'd been doing some thinking along these same lines. See chapter 7, "Avoiding Cone-Shaped Hackle Collars," for instructions on creating bushier hackle collars that won't twist your tippet.

Theories are great because they beg more questions: Have we demanded too much from hackle growers? Are we overhackling our flies with too many turns of high-density hackle? Is softer hackle better? Have we reached a point of overkill on hackle density and stiffness? I'm beginning to think so. Lately I've been asking myself, "How good is good enough?" My answer is to stay with what works best for me, which is #3 necks.

Or we could all take up nymph fishing and not have to worry about any of this!

SIX

Hackle Sizing

※

I size all my dry-fly hackle with a hackle gauge. I usually scalp an entire neck or two, depending on how many flies I'm going to tie of a specific pattern. I'll pick everything from #12 down through 22 and store them in the drawers of a small-parts cabinet that I've labeled for both color and size, leaving the bottom drawer for the tailing feathers. This means I only have to spend about an hour picking and sizing hackle that will last me for a week or more of steady tying. It's pretty easy to scalp and size the hackles from a rooster neck, because the hackle fibers are almost the same length from the tip of the hackle stem to the butt. This is especially true with the high-grade genetic capes available today.

Saddles can be an entirely different matter. It's a good idea to size the entire length of each saddle feather as you pick it from the skin. I don't scalp the entire saddle, since there are usually no more than three different sizes on a high-quality skin. You'll find that many saddle feathers don't contain the same length of hackle fibers throughout the entire length of the feather. For example, the section near the butt can be a #16, the middle 3 or 4 inches will be #18, and the tip will revert to a #16. Size them carefully and break out the shorter (or longer) sections and put them in a size-marked drawer or box.

A standard practice in sizing hackle dictates that the hackle fiber length should be one and a half times the hook-gap distance for most dry flies. A few tyers insist that the proper length of the hackle fibers is twice the hook-gap distance. I think that's correct for some fly patterns; spinners seem to have longer legs than they did as duns. However, there are some tiny Baetis and Trico naturals whose legs seem to be a little shorter than they're supposed to be, according to the above rules. This is an example of insects' inability to read fly-tying books. I tie some flies with hackle fibers that are only as long as the hook-gap distance for those special hatches. You can also trim hackle collars that are too big. I have a good pair of standard fly-tying scissors attached to my vest with a heavy-duty zinger for just this reason. Sometimes I'll clip all the hackle off the bottom of a fly in order to get it to float down on the surface more like the naturals. I think it can make a difference.

Hackle sizing for parachute patterns normally requires that you use a hackle one size larger than for the same hook on a dun pattern. For example, if you were tying a #16 Adams dun, you would use hackles whose fibers were one and a half times the hook-gap distance of a #16 hook. If you were tying a #16 Adams parachute, you would use hackles whose fibers were one and a half times the hook-gap distance of a #14 hook. I'm sure you've noticed—or will notice—that when you do this, the hackle fiber tips reach the end of the abdomen and extend far beyond the hook eye. This hackle fiber configuration almost exactly matches the leg placement of the natural insect. I believe this is one reason that the parachute pattern is often more effective than a dun pattern of the same insect. Another reason is that the horizontal hackle collar allows the fly to rest on the surface more like the naturals.

Now that we're thinking about hackle fiber length in more precise terms, we should consider some other problems. Pick up any hackle gauge and you will soon discover that there's a great deal of

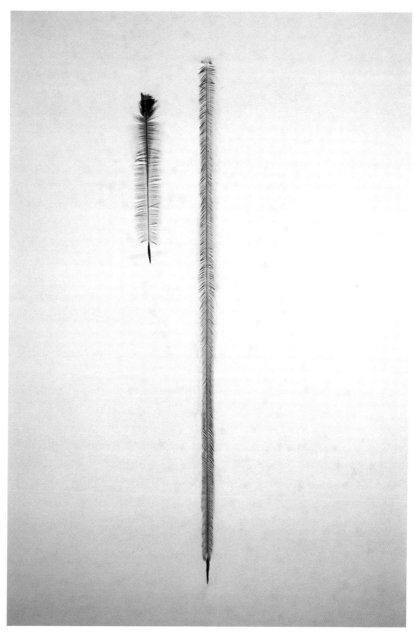

Typical genetic saddle hackle with varying hackle fiber lengths, and genetic neck hackle with one hackle fiber length

distance between one size and the next, especially in the larger sizes such as 12 and 14. A very thin line on your hackle gauge indicates that a hackle becomes a #12 at a specific point. This line is only a couple thousandths of an inch wide. Does that mean that if the hackle fibers didn't pass the line but touched the bottom of it, it's still a #14? And just when did a #14 cease being a #16? When you get into the very small hackle sizes such as 20s and 22s, does it really matter? At what point can you stop fudging with the hackle fiber length? If a hackle fiber length is 2/1000 inch short of being a #12, is your fly a poorly tied fly? More importantly, do the trout even care? But then again, if leg length and placement are so important to the overall appearance of the fly, why not attempt to imitate the natural as accurately as possible?

Does all this mean that we need to size hackles in half sizes? There are a few hooks available that come in all the odd sizes and I've never understood why they haven't become more popular, since insects don't seem to understand that they're supposed to come in even-sized hook proportions only. How many times have you fished a hatch with a #18 dry fly only to discover that it was too small, and you should really be fishing a 17 because a 16 was too big? Tying on these odd-sized hooks would solve the problem of how to use those hackles that are too big to be an 18 and too small to be a 16, and you'd have a fly that more accurately imitated the natural from a proportional standpoint.

I wind a lot of hackle measured to match the natural's proportions, not some iron-clad rule that a #17 blue-winged olive hasn't seen. There are some good guidelines to follow in fly tying, but they are only that, guidelines. It is perfectly acceptable to stray from them. For example, I once saw a fly tied to imitate the large western green drake. It was tied on a #14 short-shank hook and had a beautifully constructed extended body of two colors of deer hair ribbed with another color of thread, split tails, and an exquisite pair of wings cocked in just the correct manner—but it was hackled with #14 hackle! The western green drake is a huge mayfly with prominent long legs that is normally tied on a #12 hopper hook such as Mustad 94831, or a Tiemco 5262 #12. The tyer had assumed that he was required to use #14 hackle because he was tying on a #14 hook. There are guidelines devised by people, and absolutes devised by nature. Tie them the way they look to *you*.

Just when we think we're getting close to solving problems like these, some hook manufacturer comes up with a new hook style that incorporates a wider hook gap for greater hooking capacity, and through a magnificent marketing campaign convinces a huge portion of the world that this is *the* hook to use to catch more fish. My first question was, and will continue to be: Why do we need a wider gap on a #16 hook when we've been catching so many fish on #18, 20, and 22? Also, why not put the same sized gap on all smaller hooks if a wider gap on a #16 is so damn good?

In addition, if the hook gap on a new style of hook is wider, do we use the newer wider hook gap to size our hackles? I don't. I still use the hackle gauge I made years ago that was based on the hook-gap distances of Mustad 94840 dry-fly hooks. In my opinion, that hook was designed with the mayfly in mind. Nearly everything about it is in some way proportional to most of the popular mayfly hatches. I think beginning fly tyers should tie lots of flies on Mustad 94840 hooks to learn the proportions of tail length, body length, wing height, and hackle fiber length for most mayfly hatches. Then, when they become convinced that some other hook is better for whatever reason, they can make the switch and still remember how the fly should be proportioned to imitate the natural.

Commercial tyers are faced with some terrible dilemmas when it comes to all of the above. On one hand, they are expected to be able to provide flies tied on hooks that the shop owner has specified. On the other hand, commercial tyers earn their reputations by tying flies that not only look a lot like the naturals because of their silhouette, color, and proportional qualities, but also because flies are durable. When an account specifies a new hook style, tyers must adjust everything they've held to be true about how to tie a fly. Even if you're not a commercial tyer, you face the same set of dilemmas.

Once again we must all make some agonizing decisions. What should we do with all those old "inferior" hooks? Should we just give up dry-fly fishing? Should we just tie No-Hackle flies? I've followed my instincts. Tell yourself: "Screw 'em, I'll tie on whatever hook I want to, thank you." I've caught a hell of a lot of fish over the past thirty years on what many now consider to be inferior hooks.

SEVEN

Avoiding Cone-Shaped Hackle Collars

❋

Mayfly patterns that float downstream with their tails sticking straight up are usually the result of one or both of the following fly-tying errors: (1) The hackle collar is set too far back behind the eye of the hook, or (2) the hackle collar is cone shaped. By cone shaped, I mean the hackle fibers behind the eye are shorter than those immediately in front of the body. You can fix this problem on the stream by simply clipping the longer hackle fibers from the bottom of the collar back a bit. I like to do this anyway, just to get the fly closer to the surface. Clipping the hackle from the bottom of the fly will also prevent tippet twist.

Most fly-tying instructions tell us to attach the wings with the tips forward over the eye. We are then directed to tie the hackle butt over the wing butts. The sum of the two tie-ins will increase the diameter behind the wings by up to 60 percent. Since most of the genetic hackle today has hackle fibers that are the same length from butt to tip, a cone-shaped hackle collar is almost guaranteed if you

Cone-shaped hackle

Straight hackle collar

tie your wings and hackle as just described. The slightest bit of tension from tippet to fly will cause the fly to tip tail up.

Try the following to avoid a cone-shaped hackle collar:

1. Save a space in front of the body equal to about three to four hook-eye lengths for wings, hackle, and head.
2. Tie in the hen hackle tip wings with the tips pointing to the *rear.* Place them slightly on your side of the hook and allow thread torque to slide them to the top of the shank. Lean them forward and figure-eight-wrap to an upright position.
3. Trim a hackle butt and tie it on *in front* of the wings with the dull side up. Attach your hackle pliers to the hackle tip and make the first turn of hackle away from you in front of the far wing, down and up behind the wings. The hackle feather should twist, which allows the fibers to lean to the rear. Take one or two more turns of hackle (depending on hook size) behind the wings, and cross the hackle forward *under* the wings for hackle wraps in front of the wings. The hackle feather should twist again, allowing the fibers to lean forward. Never wrap hackle between the wings. Always try to achieve one-third hackle behind and two-thirds hackle in front of the wings.

Tying both the wing butts and the hackle butt in front of the wings will cause the diameter of the hackle collar in front of the wings to be equal to the diameter of the hackle behind the wings, which prevents a cone-shaped hackle collar. Other advantages are that the hackle fibers lean both forward and backward like the legs of the live insect, and there can be no turbine effect since the hackle fibers are facing opposite directions.

First twist

Second twist

EIGHT

Heads

———————————— ✳

The head is that portion of the fly where the final knot is made after the tyer has completely tied the rest of the fly. You could argue that the trimmed deer-hair body of a bass bug is the head of the fly, but there is always a final knot, and *that* is the head. The final knot is some distance behind the eye of the hook on flies such as the Bullet Head Hopper and the Thunder Creek Streamer series, but this knot is still part of the head and must be finished carefully.

The primary function of the head on any fly is to form a knot that prevents the fly from coming apart. Secondary functions include covering and holding the butts of the last materials tied to the hook firmly in place. The heads on streamers may serve as platforms to which you may apply stick-on eyes or model enamel paint, which you should overcoat with a layer of lacquer or epoxy to protect them. Heads can also serve as water pushers on streamers that attract fish with underwater vibrations as they are retrieved through the water. Function is also determined to some degree by pattern requirements, whether you're tying a fly designed by someone else and you want to faithfully reproduce it, the fly is for display purposes, or it's for use.

Before tying the first piece of material to the hook of any fly pattern, the first considerations should be the size and shape of the head. In some cases, one will determine the other. Generally speaking, I like to save one hook-eye distance for the head space on all my standard trout dry, wet, and nymph flies in #12 through 26. On larger flies such as Green Drakes, Stonefly Nymphs, and adults, I often save a space equal to one and a half times the hook-eye distance, since these flies have prominent heads. Hook-eye distance is defined by the space measured from the leading outside edge of the hook eye to the beginning of the hook shank.

Down-eye or up-eye hooks don't affect the shape of the head, since heads are completed immediately behind the hook eye. Although the hook eye may be considered part of the "head" of the fly (baitfish), it's merely a place to which the leader is attached, and as such is necessary. Traditionally tied full-dress salmon flies had no eyes, but a length of leader was tied to the hook shank. The thread head of the fly ended precisely at the end of the hook wire.

The size and shape of heads on streamers will be determined by the materials tied to the hook at the shoulder of the fly as well as the final wing, topping, hackle, or throat of the fly and how you cut off the butts of these final materials. There are many books readily available that clearly explain how to determine the shape of heads on large streamers such as Mickey Finns, Gray Ghosts, or Deceivers. If you read the instructions carefully and follow them precisely, you will soon be able to create nicely shaped and proportioned heads on all your streamers. Always remember that large amounts of material tied to the hook will result in large heads. A sparsely tied streamer will always have a proportionally smaller head.

Head size and shape are also determined by the size and kind of tying thread you use. I'm a strong believer in using the heaviest and strongest tying thread on flies that are to be fished. For example, I never use 8/0 tying thread until I begin tying on #24 and smaller hooks. It's at that size that 6/0 begins to build up too much bulk in the body and the heads become too big. Fine threads have less surface contact with the materials and therefore require a few more turns to firmly attach them to the hook. Since I am a compulsive time-saver when it comes to tying flies, I like to save a few seconds every chance I get. It only takes five to seven turns of 6/0 thread to securely attach anything to the hook of a standard #12 to 22 trout fly. However, the thread tension should be near the breaking point to accomplish this. If you aren't occasionally breaking the thread, you're not tying with enough thread tension.

Some threads are twisted and some are flat, which will affect the size and shape of the head. You can create either by spinning the bobbin. Twisted threads can flatten as you wrap them, because you're unwinding the twist with each revolution of the bobbin. I like flat thread when I'm tying on tail fibers and body material; then at the head I'll give the bobbin a good spin to twist the thread before I whip-finish. This seems to make the thread slightly stronger, it doesn't fray as easily, and my heads are firmer and neater.

Some tarpon flies such as the Cockroach utilize the forward three-fourths of the hook shank as the head. It's really pretty when it's done right. I like to start the thread immediately behind the eye using Danville's Flat Waxed Nylon. I use the tag as a thread guide as I completely cover the hook shank with neat tight wraps to the beginning of the hook bend. Then I tie in the wings and hackle collar. After clipping off the hackle tips, I wind the thread all the way to the eye and back to the leading edge of the hackle collar, where I whip-finish. Use your thumbnail as a thread guide as you make these final two layers of thread to the eye and back. It seems to take three layers of thread to prevent the hook shank from showing through, especially after applying lacquer or epoxy—which will always give the thread a degree of translucency.

It's desirable to have a finished head as smooth as glass. If you use lacquer, it'll take at least five coats to accomplish this. It's beautiful, but takes one or two days. Or you can use five-minute epoxy and have dry heads in less than half a day. In either case, you'll need to devise some sort of drying rack or slowly rotating wheel or drum to allow the heads to dry without sagging.

I made my own drying wheel by using a 16-rpm motor from Flex Coat. Pull the black bulb-shaped gadget off the shaft and discard. It's for holding a rod butt while rod windings dry. Remove the

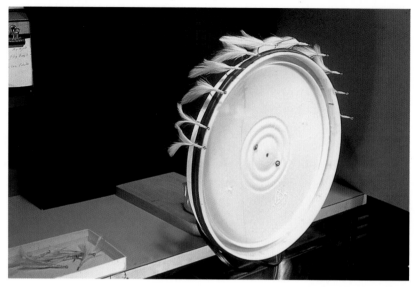

Drying drum

motor from its mount on the stand and place it on the other side of the stand. This will provide more clearance between the stand and the wheel you'll attach to the shaft later. Mount the stand centered on one end of a piece of oak ¾ inch thick by 6 inches wide by 12 inches long. Trim the corners of the board back about 3 inches from the edges of the metal stand to provide clearance for the wheel. Get a plastic lid from a 5-gallon paint can and drill a one-quarter-inch hole in the exact center. Get a cheap 5-inch fan blade that has a collar with a one-quarter-inch hole and an Allen screw in the collar. Center the fan blade over the hole in the paint can lid and drill holes in the blades and lid to accept some short pop rivets. Pop-rivet the fan blade to the lid and attach to the motor shaft. Next, get some rubber weatherstripping that is open on one edge so that the end view looks like a skinny letter *u*. It should be about five-eighths inch wide. Glue the weatherstripping in a continuous length around the side of the lid with Barge Cement. Tape it down with masking tape and let it dry overnight. Remove the masking tape and you'll have a drying wheel that doesn't deteriorate each time you remove a hook (such as it would if made with cork or foam), and holds six dozen

#4/0 Deceivers at a time. It will also firmly hold #6/0 tarpon flies. One word of caution before you glue the weatherstripping to the wheel: You must decide if you want to push your flies into the open side of the strip from the front of the wheel or pull them in from the back side. Plug the power cord into a power strip with an on/off switch or install an in-line on/off switch on the power cord.

I visited Bob Marriot's fly-fishing store in Fullerton, California, a few years ago and checked out the head cements offered. He stocks twenty-four different varieties and/or brands of head cement, not counting Sally Hansen's Hard as Nails. However, I use a high-gloss, fast-drying lacquer from the hardware store. It's still the best head cement money can buy. At $9 a quart, it's the most economical and extremely durable. A pint of thinner costs about $2. So for $11, you'll have a lifetime supply of head lacquer for yourself and a couple of buddies. Thin it for greater penetration or let it thicken for glossy heads on streamers.

In conclusion, the head is probably the most important part of any fly. If it fails, the fly will come apart. Learn to whip-finish using a minimum of five turns, and use the best head cement or lacquer available to seal the knot.

NINE

Tying Yourself Out of Trouble

✳

"*Damn!*" "*Arghh!*" "*Echh!*" and other assorted guttural sounds can be periodically heard from the row of invited fly tyers at every fly-fishing show in the country. We've all heard them. In fact, we've all made disgusted sounds in the privacy of our homes when something went dramatically wrong at precisely the right time. It can be the thread, the hackle, the wings, the quill, or any one of a dozen things that break, crack, twist, or get cut off by accident before you finish tying the fly. "Now what'll I do?" is usually the first thought that comes to mind. Most of the answers are little more than common sense, but there are a few extra tricks you can utilize to salvage a fly and tie yourself out of trouble.

You'll need a few extra tools that ought to be in your tool drawer anyway. The first thing you need to do is get them out of the drawer and hang them on pushpins for instant access. You don't always have the luxury of time to search through a drawer to find a pair of hemostats. The extra tools you must have are:

1. Small straight hemostats.
2. Extra hackle pliers (English-style).
3. Razor blade or X-Acto knife (hard to hang on a pushpin).
4. Tacky tying wax.
5. Tweezers.
6. Magnet on a string.

THREAD BREAKS WHILE SPINNING DEER HAIR

I hate it when that happens. Should it occur while you're spinning the first clump of hair, simply remove the loose clump by unwinding the broken thread. Grasp the broken tag with hemostats and let it hang. The weight will provide enough tension to prevent the thread from unwinding. Restart the tying thread, being careful to keep the remaining hook shank bare. Do not clip off the thread tags, because you may break the thread again. Tie on a *smaller* clump of hair. Most of the time the thread breaks because you're attempting to spin a clump of hair that's about twice the size it should be.

Thread breaks while spinning deer hair

If the thread breaks while spinning the second or third clump of hair, immediately press the hair bundle tightly to the hook with your left-hand forefinger. Grasp the broken tag with your hemostat to maintain tension and rethread the bobbin (the thread usually shoots back to the spool). Wind the tag forward of the bundle and take one or two turns around the hook shank. Restart your tying thread over the broken tag and then make two or three firm turns through the bundle. Pack it tightly with a hair packer, apply a tiny drop of head lacquer, and continue. If there isn't enough tag length to accomplish this, you'll have to unwind the last bundle and then restart the thread. *Do not* cut off the tags until you've finished the fly.

THREAD BREAKS WHILE SPINNING OR WRAPPING A DUBBING LOOP

The thread usually breaks at the point where it's looped through the tool and is caused by twisting it too many times. Immediately grasp the broken portion with your thumb and forefinger and transfer the

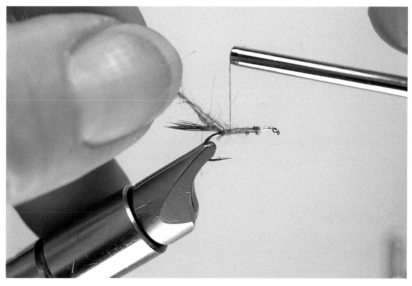

Thread breaks while spinning or wrapping a dubbing loop

broken ends to a hackle pliers. Reapply any lost twists and continue. If the thread should break where it's attached to the hook, immediately grasp the broken ends with your thumb and forefinger. Apply pressure to the material already on the hook with your third finger, use the tying thread from the bobbin to attach the broken loop as if it were a piece of yarn, and continue.

THREAD BREAKS AT ANY OTHER TIME

You need to know how strong your tying thread is. If it doesn't break once in a while, you're not tying with enough thread tension, and your flies will come apart. When the thread does break, immediately anchor it and any material already on the hook with your left forefinger (if you're right-handed), grasping the end attached to the hook with a pair of hemostats or hackle pliers. Either of these tools will prevent the thread from unwinding while you rethread the bobbin and restart the thread over the tag. Clip off both tags and continue. A well-waxed thread takes a set as you tie and helps prevent the loose tag from unwinding.

THREAD FRAYS

This is usually caused by rough skin, nicking the thread on the hook point, or because the bobbin tube has a tiny nick at the open end. Simply wrap a short frayed section (½ to 1 inch) up the hook shank and back. Make a loop of a longer frayed section as you would a dubbing loop and clip the loop off. Be careful that your tying thread is securely anchored before you cut the loop away.

BOBBIN TUBE IS FRAYING THREAD

Remove the tying spool of thread from the bobbin and replace it with a spool of Kevlar thread. Thread the Kevlar through the tube, grasp the tag end with your left thumb and forefinger, and rotate the bobbin with the same motion you'd use in wrapping thread on a

Thread frays, loop

hook shank. Use lots of tension, and keep the angle between the thread and the bobbin tube at 90 degrees or more. If you notice the Kevlar thread beginning to fray, pull a little more thread through the tube and repeat until there's no more fraying. Rotate the bobbin 180 degrees and repeat the process. The strong Kevlar fibers will polish the inside edge of the end of your bobbin tube and remove any tiny nicks or faults that fray 6/0 and 8/0 thread. Alternatively, you could just get a new bobbin.

WINGS TWIST WHILE HACKLING

There are only three reasons that this might happen. The first is that the wings are not firmly attached to the hook and the entire wing assembly twists as you begin to wrap the hackle. In this case, remove the hackle, take four or five very firm turns of tying thread over the wing tie-down area, and apply a drop of head lacquer. The second and third reasons this might happen are that the hackle stem is tied

Bobbin tube is fraying thread

too close to the base of the wing, or there isn't enough space for another turn of hackle where you'd like to make it. A hackle stem that is too close to the base of the wing will push one wing out of position or (in the case of hen hackle tip wings) cause one wing to twist by trapping a few fibers at its base. Use your bodkin to push the tiny fibers away from the hackle as you continue to wrap.

HACKLE STEM BREAKS

The solution to this problem depends on how much of the hackle remains. You may find that there is enough of the butt end of the hackle to make four or more turns of hackle. Four or five turns of hackle on a #16 or smaller hook is usually enough to complete the fly. A fuller hackle collar can be made by tying in a shorter hackle after you've tied off the broken one. Some hackles have extremely fine quills that break off just when you're ready to tie off the tip. Quickly press your left-hand forefinger against the hackle collar and bring the tying thread back into the hackle collar to anchor the work you've already done, then apply a full head and whip-finish. I always try to salvage as much as I can, but sometimes it's best simply to begin again with a new hackle.

Hackle stem breaks

QUILLS CRACK

You should always tie with a thread that's the same color as the quills or one shade lighter. Size 16 and larger flies require two quills to build a natural body taper. There's no need to be concerned if the leading smaller-diameter quill cracks, since the thicker quill that follows will cover the cosmetic flaw. The larger quill may crack in one or two places. This may happen on smaller flies as well as where only one quill is required to construct a finely tapered body. Simply wrap the tying thread in close (but slightly open) spiral wraps back over the cracks and then forward again to prevent the body from coming apart on the first fish. Cover this portion of the fly with thin head lacquer. Quills that separate along the length of the quill should be removed and replaced. Cracked quills may be the result of not soaking them long enough in water before use. Five to ten minutes is usually enough. There will always be some cracked quills, because the feathers are handled many times before you get them. Split quills are caused by too much time in the bleach-and-water solution that removed the hackle fibers. No amount of extra soaking time can fix them.

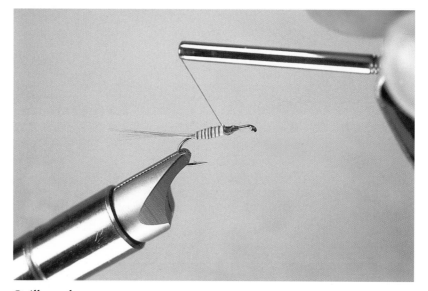

Quills crack

BIOT IS TOO SHORT FOR BODY LENGTH

Tie the biot to the hook as you normally would. Bring the thread forward to midshank. Begin wrapping the biot and, when you reach midshank, wrap both biot and thread at the same time, being certain that the thread is always on top of the biot. Each turn of biot is held down by a turn of thread. This technique will also prevent the biot from completely unwinding should it get cut by a trout's tooth. And it allows you to tie off the biot with a minimum of turns. Once again, use a thread that is the same color as the biot. See chapter 14, "Indestructible Biots," for further information.

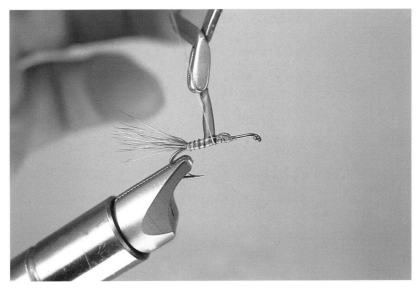

Biot is too short

DUBBED BODY IS BUMPY

There are a couple of ways to smooth a bumpy body. (Exercise?) Spiral-wrap the tying thread back toward the tail and forward again to the shoulder, making sure that where the threads cross is over a high spot. It's quick. Another method is to spiral-wrap the thread back to the thinnest portion and apply a very thin layer of dubbing to fill in the low spots. The best method, of course, is to pay close attention as you build a dubbed body and you'll have no problems. Always be certain that the dubbing rope is smooth and slender.

HOOK EYE IS OPEN

Sometimes I don't notice this until I'm ready to tie in the hackle. The quickest method to solve this problem is to lash the end of a

Bumpy body and applying thread wrap on it

trimmed hackle butt against the side of the hook and close the gap with the end of the hackle stem. Hackle over the lashed-down stem and no one will ever know what you did.

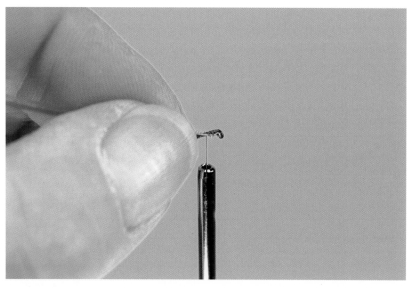

Hook eye is open

TAIL IS CANTED TO ONE SIDE OR CURVED DOWN

A tail that's canted to one side usually indicates that you didn't use enough thread tension when tying the tail in place. It happens as you begin to build the body, which will either twist the tail or push it to one side. Grip the rear of the body and the tail with your thumbnail and forefinger and twist it back. Then push the tail up with your thumbnail and apply a tiny drop of thin head lacquer. This will bleed into the thread wraps and keep the tail in position. Curved-down tails are usually caused by wrapping the rear of the body into the hook bend. Try to slide the tail and rear portion of the body back onto the hook shank with your thumbnail and forefinger, applying a tiny drop of head lacquer to secure it in place. Use maximum thread tension when tying in moose-, elk-, or deer-hair tailing material.

Curved tail

DROPPED A #24 IN THE WASTE TROLL!

Every tyer should have a small horseshoe magnet on a string that can be dangled into the waste troll bag to retrieve dropped hooks and flies. Once, I spilled a thousand #22 hooks. Half of them landed on the carpeted floor. I got all of them with the magnet, which was strong enough so that even if a hook was caught in the carpet, the magnet would cling to it and show me where it was. It will also magnetize the tip of your dubbing needle, which will help you pick those tiny hooks from the box.

WING CASE SLIPS OUT AT TIE-DOWN *AFTER* YOU'VE CLIPPED OFF THE BUTT

There are only two ways to solve this problem. One is to unwind the thorax and apply a new quill segment for the wing case. The second method is to press the slipped-out portion into place with your left forefinger nail and attempt to catch the end with tying thread. The result may be a little larger head than you anticipated, but it does sometimes work and saves a little time. Most natural nymphs have larger heads than is stylistically acceptable by a lot of tyers.

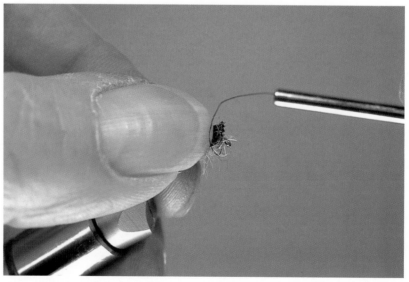

Fixing a slipped-out wing case

STRAY HACKLE OR TAIL FIBERS

You need a good pair of tweezers and a sharp X-Acto knife, razor blade, or scissor blade. Grasp the end of the stray fiber with the tweezer, lift it up, and slice it off as close as possible to the point where it's anchored. The surrounding fibers will merely bend out of the way.

Slicing off a stray tail fiber

NOT ENOUGH ROOM FOR THE HEAD

This is a common problem among inexperienced tyers. A crowded head almost always results in a whip-finish that covers half the hook eye and bends the last turn of hackle to the rear. It's also the head that always comes apart. Try using your right thumbnail to compress the final assembly (usually the hackle collar) to the rear by only 2/1000 or 3/1000 inch. This requires very firm pressure of the thumbnail directly on the hook wire immediately in front of the thread wraps. Whip-finish and apply two coats of thin head lacquer.

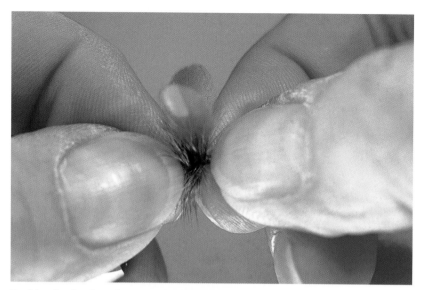

Pushing back when there's no head space

Here are a few general rules to prevent some of the troubles listed above:

1. Always tie with the strongest and largest thread that hook size will allow.
2. Always tie with maximum thread tension.
3. Pay absolute attention to every tiny detail.
4. Always attempt to tie the perfect fly.

TEN

Delicate Flies
for Skinny Water

✳

You fished your favorite stretch of river hard all day, had a couple of fair hatches, and managed to land a fair number of trout by doing everything right. Then, as you're considering calling it a day, some rise forms become visible near the tail of a long, slow, shallow glide or glass-smooth pool. It's a place where you hardly ever see a trout the rest of the day. But as dusk begins to settle in, trout magically begin feeding in water so shallow, your boot tops wouldn't get wet. It's a dry-fly fisher's dream come true. That last magic hour or two of an already successful day. Wouldn't catching a nice trout here just be the icing on the cake?

In a situation like this, you must rebuild your leader to 12 or 15 feet with 30 or 40 inches of 7X tippet, maybe even 8X. Your approach must be as stealthy as a heron's. Your casting position must be perfect, and your first cast must present the fly as delicately as thistledown. Your imitation must slowly drift with all the freedom of the naturals down to what may be the biggest trout of the day.

You look through your fly boxes and find no fly as delicate in appearance as the naturals you see on the water. All you can find are heavily hackled, much-used, bulky, ragged flies that just don't look right.

All you can do is give it your best shot and promise yourself to learn how to tie dainty flies, because you're probably not going to find many of the following patterns in your local fly shop. These are the sparsely dressed, delicate patterns that have been very useful when I've been lucky enough to find trout rising in skinny water. You won't need more than two or three of each pattern, which you should keep in a separate fly box. You won't need more of these flies, because you'll probably get no more than one cast per pool. One strike and hookup with a trout will usually put the entire pool down until the next day.

My definition of *skinny water* is any water that's just barely deep enough to hold fish. You can see their dorsal fins as they cruise around in shallow backwaters or hold at the tail end of a large pool. Sit down and watch for a while to determine how many fish there are when you see them rising in these places. A backwater pool may contain only one or two fish, or it could be as many as three or four, depending on the size of the area. Get into a position to see them without spooking them and watch for a cruising pattern. A fish in a backwater seldom holds in one spot. Like any good hunter, it will be looking for food by slowly cruising in a circular pattern, which could be clockwise or counterclockwise. Pick the largest fish, because you're probably only going to get one shot at it; if a smaller fish eats your fly first, the big guy is gone! Then try to see if you can spot the areas where it most often rises. You'll be able to see the flies it's eating if you're really lucky. Plan your casting position, the exact spot where you think the fly ought to land, and try to visualize the drift to the trout. This will occasionally require you to cast behind the fish and wait for it to come around again.

Several trout rising near the tail of a large pool will require some painful decisions. Do you cast to the larger fish in the center and take the chance of "lining" the smaller fish between you and the big guy, which could spook the entire pool? Or do you cast to the smaller fish near you and hope you can land them without spooking the big guy in the center? I usually opt for the smaller fish first, in the belief that it's better to land one small fish than none. This is an excellent time to play a hooked fish with your rod to one side and parallel to the surface in the hope that you can pull it away from the other rising fish and prevent it from jumping. You can usually muscle a small fish away and play it out to one side of the stream.

It's a safe bet that these trout are sipping spinners, cripples, or another pattern that I call the Clumsy Dun—flies that have simply fallen to one side and have one wing stuck in the surface film. Another pattern that works well is the NQ (Not Quite) Spinner: a spinner that alights on the surface with its clear wings in an upright position. Observe the rise forms. Tiny little dimples on the surface often indicate that the trout are taking spinners. Watch for a rise form that includes a bulge in the water before you see the dimple. It could be a very large fish. You must always remember one very important thing in this situation: Large trout can go wherever they please, and they like to feed in places that require a minimum amount of effort. It's not unusual to find huge trout in skinny water, especially on overcast days or in the evening.

You'd be wise to sample the water with a bug net well upstream to determine what insects are being washed into the feeding area. Pay particular attention to the number of bugs you net, what phase of their life cycle you're seeing more of, and their exact color and size. Compare what you find in your bug net to the rise forms you have been observing, and you will have narrowed the possibilities dramatically. There is a good chance that a small red or black ant or winged beetle will work if there's no hatch or spinner fall and the rises you have spotted are occasional.

Trout that rise in skinny water always seem to be feeding on small flies. Tying small flies requires a major change in what you *think* you can accomplish. I've met a lot of people who have watched me tie a #24 Olive Quill Dun and said, "I could never do that. Hell, I can't even see the hook." Or, "When the flies get that small I just quit fishing, 'cause I can't see the fly on the water anyway." That bothers me, because most of us got into the sport of fly fishing with open minds, willing to learn something new. Then somehow these folks formed a few iron-clad opinions and probably will happily fish a #16 Adams through a #22 Trico hatch and claim they can't catch many fish because of their rod. It's no more difficult to tie a #24 dry fly than it is to tie a #14. It can even be argued that it's easier and faster—the smaller fly requires less material and fewer turns of thread, and you can only make tiny mistakes.

The biggest problem most people have in tying small flies is proportion. The answer to this is simple. The proportions are the same as larger flies. If you use fewer turns of thread to tie down material, you'll have a chance at becoming a very good small-fly tyer. That said, there are some species of late-season blue-winged olives that have oversized wings and shorter-than-normal length tails. Catch a few naturals next time you go fishing in the fall, and notice the proportions. The trout will often key in on this feature, and even though you have a fly tied on the right-sized hook, the wings will be too short—and you'll go fishless. Compare the wing length to the body length of the natural. You'll occasionally find a BWO whose wings are longer than the entire body, including the tails!

Proportion applies to more than just wing height and tail length. It also dictates body diameter and hackle length. You can hardly tie a small fly with a body diameter that's too thin. This is a very important point to keep in mind, because a body that's too fat will inevitably cause you to tie the rest of the fly out of proportion. Tie in a tail that contains only three or four spade hackle fibers. If you use more than that, you'll begin to build up an underbody that is too bulky. I prefer to use stripped and dyed rooster hackle quills for the bodies of all my small mayfly imitations, because I think it's easier to achieve the tiny body diameters needed to imitate the naturals. Use the smallest-diameter quills you can find for this. Dubbed-body flies must be carefully constructed: Use only a few fibers at a time as you dub the material onto the thread. Use thread that is lighter than the dubbing, and press the dubbing on very firmly. Try to avoid a fuzzy body. See the section on "Silk Dubbing" on page 87.

The legs on the tiny naturals will often be shorter than you'd expect. Hackle length isn't very important in supporting your fly on the surface when you're tying tiny flies for skinny water. You could probably tie the fly without any hackle and it would work just fine.

I just have to see hackle on a dry fly—after all, mayflies do have legs. You only need two to three turns of hackle on #20 to 26 dry flies. More than that would be too much. I try to keep it to three or four turns on a #18.

Keep in mind that trout couldn't care less whether or not you like to tie tiny flies. When #24 BWOs are on the water, that's all they're interested in eating. The difference between the length of a #24 hook and a #26 hook is only about 2/1000 inch. I fished the South Platte River recently with Mike Clark during a hatch of tiny BWOs. I cast a #24 Olive Quill Dun to a rising fish for nearly half an hour without success. I was hesitant to change flies because I had been catching fish on the same fly. There were still duns on the water, and I could see my trout eat them. In desperation, I tied on a tiny #26—and the trout ate it on the first cast. It was only then that I netted the water and discovered that the hatch had changed. Remember what I said earlier about "iron-clad" ideas? I was so convinced that I had on the right-sized fly that I didn't bother to check.

Here's a tip for fishing tiny flies: Tie on a #16 Blond Caddis, then tie an 18-inch dropper off the bend of the Caddis and tie a tiny fly to the end of the dropper. The larger Caddis will help you "find" your tiny fly. You may even discover that one or two trout will attack your Caddis. Always use 7X when fishing any fly smaller than a #20 so the fly will float more freely.

My favorite fly patterns for fishing skinny water are:

RED QUILL SPINNER

These quill-bodied mayfly spinners with hen hackle tip wings and tails are very sparsely tied with the stiffest spade hackle I can find. I tie all my spinners with tails that are at least twice as long as the entire hook and widely splayed. I like to hackle spinners of #16 and larger with only three widely spaced wraps of hackle through the thorax area and then clip the bottom of the collar flush with the dubbed thorax.

Hook: Mustad 94840 or Tiemco 100, size to match natural. On #18 and smaller hooks, I prefer to use either ring-eye or up-eye hooks.

Hackled spinner

Thread: Danville's 6/0 #41 or 429 tan. Use 8/0 or finer on #18 and smaller hooks.

Tail: Small clump of ginger or light brown very stiff spade hackle fibers, length to equal two times hook length, tied splayed.

Body: One stripped and light tan dyed rooster hackle quill. Make all spinner bodies as slender as possible.

Wings: Pair of white hen hackle tips, tied spent. Use Sparkle Organza fibers for the wings on hooks #22 and smaller. (See instructions below.)

Thorax: Fine dry-fly dubbing a shade darker than the quill.

Hackle: Two or three turns of very stiff dark ginger or light brown hackle. Omit the hackle on #18 and smaller hooks.

ORGANZA SPINNER WINGS

Finding a good winging material for spinners is a problem that tyers have had to deal with for a long time. I dislike using poly yarn because it always ends up looking like a small pillow on the water, no matter how much I separate, stretch, and wax it. On spinners #20

Sparkle Organza Spinner wings

and larger, I can usually find some passable white hen hackle tips for wings. But for #22 and smaller hooks, finding good winging material is a genuine challenge. These are tiny little spinners that usually begin to fall a little before dusk and whose wings are so clear, they're almost invisible. It's what drove me to a fabric shop about fifteen years ago in search of some kind of material I might be able to use for spinner wings.

You can find White Sparkle Organza at most large fabric shops. Purchase the smallest amount you can. I found a fabric shop that gave me some samples. You may have to buy a yard of it, but that's okay—you'll have a lifetime supply for yourself, your kids, and your grandkids. Cut the material into three or four 4-inch squares and store the rest.

1. Tie the spinner tail and body as usual, being sure to extend the body well into the thorax area, which will provide a wide enough area to attach the wing fibers.

2. Strip off three fibers from one side of the 4-inch-square piece, cut them in half, and tie three 2-inch fibers to one side of the

hook. Take one turn of thread over the center of the fibers and pull the six ends to the side to position them. Take a second turn of thread exactly over the first turn to anchor the fibers in place. Repeat for the other side of the hook.

Organza fibers tied in

3. Figure-eight the fibers with tying thread so the six horizontal fibers on each side of the hook are slightly fanned. Apply a small drop of head lacquer to the center of each wing to help them stay in this position.

4. Apply some fine dry-fly dubbing firmly to the tying thread. Silk dubbing is ideal here (see "Silk Dubbing" on page 87).

5. Create a small dam of dubbing both in front of and behind the wing fibers.

6. Figure-eight the dubbing only in front of and behind the two dubbing dams. *Never* allow the figure-eight dubbing to touch the wing fibers: It will compress them, and they'll look like two shiny sticks.

Dubbing dams

Figure-eight dubbing in front of and behind the dams

7. Trim the wings. Each wing should be equal to the length of the entire hook. It's helpful to make a template that you can hold against the side of the body of the fly under each wing to get them even. Slide the bottom scissor blade between the wing and the template to trim. I like to trim the trailing fibers just a bit shorter than the leading-edge fibers for a more accurate wing shape.

Trimming the wing fibers

TINY CINNAMON ANTS

A lot of fly fishers always carry a few red or black ant patterns in their fly boxes. But I've noticed the smallest size they have is seldom less than a #20. The problem with this is that there are a lot of smaller ants, especially cinnamon ants, that somehow end up in the stream. Trout must like them a lot, because they'll often eat an ant pattern during a BWO hatch or spinner fall. Skinny water seems to make a #22 or 24 Cinnamon Ant even more delectable.

Hook: #20 through 24 Mustad 94842 or Tiemco 101.
Thread: 8/0 or finer tan.

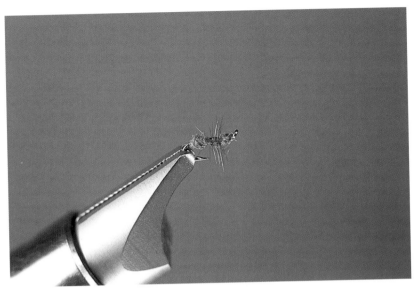

#22 Cinnamon Ant

Body: Small ball of silk dubbing tightly dubbed and wound on the hook in a reverse teardrop shape. Do not dub beyond the hook point! Note: See the section below on "Silk Dubbing."

Hackle: Two turns of very stiff light brown hackle.

Head: Tiny ball of silk dubbing tightly dubbed just behind the hook eye.

SILK DUBBING

The secret to using silk dubbing is to pinch off very tiny tufts that you will twist tightly onto the thread to make the dubbing rope. A good way to judge what constitutes a tiny tuft is to compare it to the top of a dandelion seed, then use half of that. Stroke your forefinger on some dubbing wax before twisting the dubbing onto the thread. The first pinch of dubbing shouldn't change the diameter of the thread by more than 50 percent, and should taper down to the thread diameter.

Be sure that the top of each additional pinch of dubbing overlaps the bottom of the previous application. This should be the rule

Tiny tuft of silk dubbing

in the use of any dubbing, but it's especially the case with silk dubbing. Think of it as impregnating the thread with dubbing when you twist it on as tightly as you can. *Always* attempt to get most of the fibers at a 90-degree angle to the thread, which will ensure that each fiber wraps completely around the thread. When you align the dubbing fibers parallel with the tying thread, it will only create a dubbing rope next to the thread.

Silk dubbing compresses so well that you might want to consider using it on all dry flies #18 and smaller. I also recommend using 8/0 or finer thread that's as close to the dubbing color as possible. If you can't get a good match, always choose a lighter-colored thread.

WINGED BEETLES

My favorite beetle pattern has two small oval-shaped dun hackle tips extending from the rear, a shellback of bronze Bugskin, a chocolate-dubbed body, and brown palmer hackle clipped flush with the bottom of the body.

#24 BWO with silk-dubbed body

All the beetle patterns I've seen are beautifully tied versions of a perfect beetle. Everything about them is as anatomically correct as a fly tyer can make them, except for one thing: A lot of the beetles that fall on the water don't look like that.

On days when there are few rises and no hatch, I spend a lot of time standing in feeding lanes, netting the water with a bug net, or lying on my belly peering over an undercut bank. I see everything from ants to houseflies. There's usually a honeybee or two, and sometimes a hornet or a wasp. However, ants and beetles seem to be the most prevalent bugs I see on these no-hatch/no-rise days.

The interesting thing about the beetles I see *on the water* is that very few of them have their wings tucked neatly away under their shells, the way they appear in all the photos where they're politely posing on a branch or colorful leaf. Most of the beetles I see on the water have a little bit of each wing tip protruding from under the rear of their shell, the way they appear just before flying away. Catch a small beetle, place it on a stick, and watch it carefully. The shell will open slightly; next, the wing tips appear, and a split second after that, they're gone. They can escape from a stick or leaf in an instant, but not from the surface of the water. They apparently don't know this and keep their wings "at the ready" just in case. It's another example in a long list of overlooked details when tying flies and photographing bugs. Sharp close-up photos of bugs floating downstream are extremely difficult to achieve. Fly tyers and photographers will capture a bug, chill it in a cooler perhaps, and then construct some artful setting for the portrait on a stick or interesting rock. By this time, the insect has completely rearranged itself for protection.

I take a lot of photos of insects while I'm fishing and figure I'm lucky if I get a usable photo from one or two rolls of film. I also carry a small spiral-bound notebook and take careful notes of exactly how the insect appears when it's *on the water*. The insects' appearances in the artful photos hardly ever match the detailed notes I made.

The exposed wing tips protruding from the rear are often 25 percent of the total profile length of the beetle. Why would we ignore this prominent feature?

Winged Bronze Beetle

> *Hook:*   Your favorite dry-fly hook, #16 through 20.
> *Thread:*   Brown 6/0 for Bronze Beetle, black 6/0 for Black Beetle.

Wing Tips: Pair of oval-shaped hen hackle tips, tied delta-wing style.

Shellback: Bronze Bugskin for Bronze Beetle, or black Bugskin for Black Beetle.

Body: Dark brown dubbing for Bronze Beetle, or black dubbing for Black Beetle.

Hackle: Dark brown palmered hackle for Bronze Beetle, or black palmered hackle for Black Beetle.

1. Attach the tying thread at midshank and wrap to the beginning of the hook bend. Twist a very small amount of dubbing onto the thread to create a tiny ball of dubbing slightly below the hook bend.

2. Select two oval-shaped hen hackle tips and tie them onto each side of the hook at the bend in a slight open-V formation. The tiny ball of dubbing will keep them separated. The tips should extend beyond the end of the bend by only half the hook-gap distance and should be level with the hook shank.

Hen hackle tips tied in

3. Cut a strip of Bugskin whose width equals the hook-gap distance and clip one end to an arrow shape.

4. Tie the Bugskin arrow tip immediately in front of the wings, shiny-side down, butt to the rear. Be careful not to displace the wings.

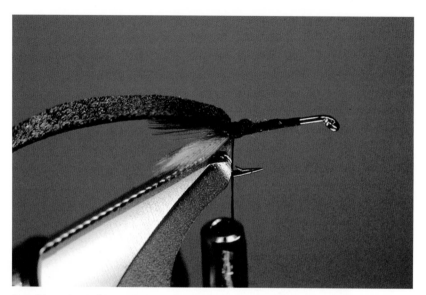

Bugskin strip tied in

5. Apply the dubbing to the thread very tightly and make one or two complete turns of dubbing immediately on top of the thread wraps that hold the Bugskin.

6. Tie in the hackle by its tip immediately in front of the ball of dubbing with the dull side facing the hook eye, and continue dubbing the remainder of the body. Save two hook-eye spaces behind the eye to tie down the materials and tie the head.

7. Wrap the hackle forward in open spirals to the front of the body, tie down, and clip off the butt.

8. Carefully trim all the hackle fibers from the top and bottom of the body.

9. Fold the Bugskin strip forward, tie it down firmly, trim away the butt, and whip-finish.

Take note of the terrestrials as you approach your favorite stream or lift a piece of rotten wood to see what's living there. Chances are the trout will be very interested in your beetle pattern if it's the same size and color, especially if it's a winged beetle.

SIMPLE FLIES

Sometimes the most technical situation calls for the simplest fly, especially in late fall, winter, and early spring, when about all you can do is dredge the bottom with nymphs. Find a midge hatch. Midges hatch nearly every day of the year. Actually, we don't find a midge hatch, the hatch finds us—but only if we notice it.

You'll soon come to realize that midge larvae and emergers drift downstream all the time. The trout are certainly accustomed to seeing and feeding on them, so why not fish subsurface midge patterns more? We're often so intent on matching the hatch that we forget to offer the trout something a little different. I think it's a good idea to fish a midge larva or an emerger as a dropper off a #18 or 20 Blue-Winged Olive during a Baetis hatch, particularly when the trout are refusing every BWO imitation you have in your fly box. I don't normally enjoy casting more than one fly at a time, but when things slow down to the point where you and your buddy haven't seen a fish in two or three hours, you can at least practice casting a two-fly setup for a while.

As a commercial tyer, I love it when one of my accounts orders a few dozen midge larvae and emergers. These are high-profit flies, because they contain only one or two pieces of material, and they are very quick to tie. For example, there's a Colorado pattern called the String Thing. It has a hook and two layers of white buttonhole twist for the body. That's it! You could finish it off with a head of black 8/0 thread if you want to get fancy and tie high-grade String Things.

I am also of the belief that we all get a little carried away with exact imitation of a very specific fly. We attempt to tie all the elbows and eyelashes of the natural onto a very small hook, and we usually end up with something that might look like an atomic-radiated bug from the year 3000. The point is, maybe it's a good idea to simplify and allow the trout to decide what the fly looks like. The String Thing mentioned above is a great example. It could be a tiny little gray worm, or a midge larva, or whatever. What we tie onto a hook is actually nothing more than a representation of an insect's appearance. Net a few bugs next time you're out on the stream, and look at them through squinted eyes. Allow your eyelashes to break up the silhouette and body colors. It'll look a little blurry, but you'll be amazed at how some details become very insignificant, others become prominent, and colors often change dramatically.

I always try to tie my flies to resemble the natural insect as closely as possible, but only to the point where I won't be tempted to shoot myself if I lose the fly on the first cast. That's why I like tying tiny midge nymphs. The completed fly consists of only four parts including the hook, and I can imitate most of the common midges with only three generic patterns tied in a number of sizes.

Rather than adding weight to these tiny patterns, I prefer to apply a small amount of lead substitute putty to the tippet about 14 inches above the fly. This gets the fly down to the depth I want and allows the tiny fly to dance around rocks with the same neutral buoyancy of the natural. The addition of any weight to the hook prior to wrapping the body material would make the fly appear too fat.

Flashabou, Krystal Flash, various colors of fine wire, and tying threads of various sizes offer a seemingly unlimited number of color combinations for the body of the fly. Catch a few of the naturals in your favorite stream and you'll be able to match them almost perfectly.

The following are three of my favorite generic midge nymphs, which I call Magic Midge Larvae.

BLACK MAGIC MIDGE LARVA

Hook: Dry fly, #14 through 22. (Use an up-eye or ring-eye hook for #18 and smaller.)

Thread: Danville black 6/0 or 8/0.

Body: Black rooster quill for #14 and 16.
Black Moose Mane for #18 and 20.
Black thread for #22 and smaller.

Black Magic Midge Larva

Thorax: One or two turns of loose black dubbing or two turns of peacock or fine black ostrich.

1. Attach the tying thread two hook-eye spaces behind the eye and wrap toward the bend with closely nested turns. For #22 and smaller hooks, bring the thread forward to within two hook-eye spaces of the eye and either dub one or two tiny turns for the thorax or attach a fine-fibered black ostrich tip and take one or two turns. Whip-finish, apply a tiny drop of head lacquer to the head, and stroke another drop of head lacquer to the thread body.

2. For #20 to 18 hooks, bring the tying thread back to within two hook-eye spaces of the eye, select two long moose mane hairs, clip off about 1 inch of the tips, and tie the remainder of the hairs to the top of the hook with their clipped tips two hook-eye spaces behind the hook eye. Wrap tying thread over the moose mane hair to the beginning of the bend, bring the thread back forward, and carefully wrap the moose mane in tight nesting wraps to the initial tie-in point. Apply one or two tiny turns of black dubbing or attach one fine-fibered black ostrich tip and

take one or two turns. Whip-finish, apply a tiny drop of head lacquer to the head, and stroke another drop of head lacquer to the moose mane body.

3. Follow the instructions in step 2 above for #16 and larger hooks. Use stripped and dyed black rooster neck hackle quills for the body.

Olive Magic Midge Larva

OLIVE MAGIC MIDGE LARVA

Hook: Dry fly, #18 through 22.

Thread: Danville light green 6/0 (four layers for body).

Ribbing: Brown 6/0
Spiral-wrap the ribbing forward, tie it over the lighter thread, cut off the lighter thread, and continue with the brown ribbing thread as tying thread for the thorax and head.

Thorax: One or two turns of loose gray rabbit dubbing or two turns of fine natural gray ostrich.

TAN MAGIC MIDGE LARVA

Hook: Dry fly, #14 through 18.

Tan Magic Midge Larva

Thread: Danville beige 6/0 (four layers for body).

Ribbing: Brown 6/0
Spiral-wrap the ribbing forward, tie it over the beige thread, cut off the beige thread, and continue with the brown ribbing thread for the thorax and head.

Thorax: Two turns of tan ostrich.

For Olive and Tan Magic Midge Larva:

1. Attach light green or beige thread to the hook about two hook-eye spaces behind the eye. Cut off the tag after only four or five turns of thread and tie in the darker (brown) ribbing thread.

2. Continue wrapping the lighter thread over the ribbing all the way to the hook bend in tightly nested wraps. Then reverse direction and wrap back toward the eye, stopping at the initial wrap. Repeat to create a four-layer thread body, and let the bobbin hang two hook-eye spaces behind the eye.

3. Spiral-wrap the ribbing forward in slightly open spirals *in the same direction as the body wraps.*

Four-layer thread body with ribbing

4. Wrap the ribbing thread over the body thread and clip off the body thread. The ribbing thread (darker thread) is now the tying thread for the remainder of the fly.

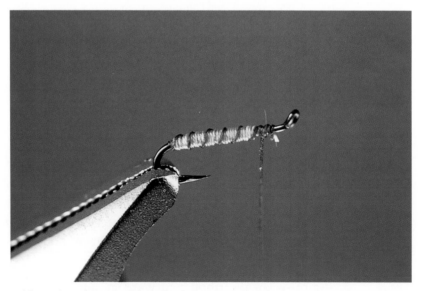

Ribbing thread as tying thread

5. Select a gray or light tan ostrich herl from near the base of the quill. Tie the base of the herl onto the hook immediately in front of the thread body. Take only two turns of herl, tie if off, clip off the tip, and whip-finish. Apply a tiny drop of head lacquer to the thread head only. Note: Select an ostrich herl whose fibers are very short. The fibers are usually shortest near the base of the herl and again near the tip. However, the herl becomes quite fragile near the tip and will break off easily when you attempt to wrap it. Trim off some of the base at a point where the herl fibers begin to become most dense and tie the remainder of the herl to the hook.

Fishing midges is one of my favorite winter activities. I'm lucky to live in Colorado, where we can fish year-round and there are many tailwater fisheries with tons of midges hatching nearly every day of the year. Between periods of surface activity, I can usually catch a few trout by drifting one of the above generic midge nymph patterns through the slower current creases and tongues. It requires a great deal of stealth and more patience than I thought I'd ever have. The payoff is often one of the largest trout I'll catch all year. It's a genuine thrill to fool an old, large, wary trout on a #20 or 22 generic midge nymph on 30 inches of 7X tippet.

PATTERN ADAPTATION

In my opinion there are only three or four patterns for trout flies: the streamer, the wet fly (is it just a tiny streamer?), the nymph, and the dry fly. I suppose we could group the streamer, wet fly, and nymph into one category and call them subsurface flies. Then we would have only two basic fly patterns, the subsurface flies and the surface flies. I realize I'm treading on dangerous ground here, because I'm not a fly-tying historian. I learned how to tie flies to save money (ho, ho) and to try to make flies that looked better than the ones I could buy when I first began to fish. This is just stuff I've been thinking about.

If a basic streamer consists of a tail, body, and some kind of wing, are all streamers simply adaptations of an original pattern? If so, maybe all dry flies are an adaptation of some original pattern consisting of tail, body, wing, and hackle collar. I remember reading an article some years ago that said today's dry flies are a relatively recent development and merely an adaptation of the original wet flies, which consisted of tail, body, wing, and hackle collar. They looked like a dry fly but didn't float. I'm of the mind that there are only two basic patterns for trout: baitfish and bugs. The rest are merely pattern adaptations. I know it's quite a stretch, because there are spinners, emergers, floating emergers, parachutes, beetles, ants, hoppers, and dozens of attractor flies. It can be argued that terrestrials blow my entire theory because there are no tails or upright wings and the tying style is completely different.

It hardly matters what any of us think about all this, because either the trout will eat our flies or they won't. What I'm getting around to is the reason we name a fly after ourselves. "A. K.'s Olive Quill Dun" is a great fly, but it's only a Blue-Winged Olive with a light green quill body. I like to think of it as a pattern adaptation that I figured out and to which I attached my name as a means of identifying my pattern alteration. There are dozens of great old patterns that we're all familiar with that can be altered or adapted to make them just a little better for our immediate needs. As long as the fly floats or sinks the way you want it to and catches fish, I think it's a legitimate thing to do.

A very popular nymph pattern in Colorado called the RS-2 has two tail fibers (split style), a thinly dubbed gray body, a short upright tuft of gray marabou in the middle of the thorax, and a black thread head. It's effective near the bottom, anyplace beneath the surface, or greased and fished in the surface film. I use it when there are no rising fish, especially in the winter when the only activity seems to be midges, but it's also very effective when a BWO hatch is about to occur. This last discovery got me to thinking. What if I made an RS-2 that more accurately resembled a floating, emerging BWO?

It's a very good idea to spend some serious time with a bug net when you set out to try to improve something that's already a pretty good fly. You need to know exactly what the natural looks like. I wanted to tie an *emerging* BWO, which meant I had to net some bugs that were partially emerged from the nymph case. The best way to do this was to put my rod in the bushes, wade out into the feeding lane, and start catching bugs. I made some interesting discoveries. The trailing shuck sparkles only when you hold it in your hand, where the sunlight reflects the wet fibers. If trout ate out of your hand, you'd be right to tie a trailing shuck with some kind of sparkling material. The trailing shucks of the naturals in the water, on the other hand, were slightly translucent, dark tan in color, visibly segmented, and short. So I wrote on a matchbook cover, "Tail: 4–5 dark tan hen back or partridge fibers." The partially emerged body was the same color as the adult and prominently segmented. I continued noting on the matchbook cover, "Body: quill as in adult." The partially emerged wing was short and curled back a bit, and I wrote on the matchbook, "Wing: short tuft of gray poly yarn for visibility."

What I ended up with was a fly that looked like an RS-2. I tie this new pattern adaptation of the RS-2 in several colors and call it the RS Quill. It's very effective in light olive (Baetis color), gray as in the original RS-2 color, cream for cream midges and some pale morning duns, and black for midges.

Original RS-2 pattern

Olive RS Quill

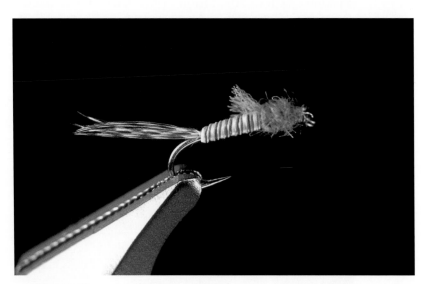

Gray RS Quill

I don't think you should arbitrarily change the color of any part of a fly and call it a pattern adaptation unless you have a legitimate reason. Changing the tail color of a Blue-Winged Olive from dun to

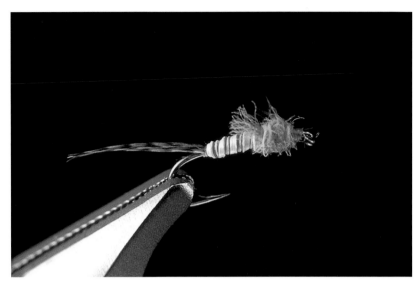

Cream RS Quill

black and then calling it a Black Tailed BWO just doesn't cut it unless you have actually found a hatch of BWOs with black tails. You can honestly say you have developed a pattern adaptation only after you determine that the trout actually prefer the black-tailed version to the dun-tailed version. Even then, you and your friends should fish this pattern adaptation for at least two or three years to determine that your adaptation is indeed a more effective fly for a specific hatch than the original.

RS QUILL

Hook:	Any dry-fly hook, #16 through 22.
Thread:	6/0 or 8/0 to match body color.
Tail:	Mottled tan hen or wood duck fibers (only four or five) for olive, cream, and black bodies. Gray mallard fibers for gray body.
Body:	Stripped and dyed rooster neck butt hackles in olive, gray, or cream.
Wing Tuft:	Light gray split poly yarn segment for all.
Thorax:	Fine medium dun dubbing for olive and gray bodies, and tan for cream bodies.

1. Start the thread on the hook immediately behind the eye and wind all the way to the bend.

2. Tie in the tailing fibers (length equal to the hook-shank length) and lash the butts to within two hook-eye lengths of the eye of the hook. Clip off the butts and leave the thread hanging at this position.

3. Tie in one stripped and dyed quill by its clipped tip (clip the tip to the diameter of the hook), and lash it down all the way to the beginning of the bend. Bring the thread forward to within two hook-eye lengths behind the hook eye.

4. Wind the quill forward in tightly nested wraps to within two hook-eye lengths, tie down, and clip off the butt.

5. Split a strand of gray poly yarn, clip the end perfectly square, and tie it in immediately in front of the shoulder of the quill body. Take two turns of thread over the butt, pull on the longer end to shorten the butt, and cover it with tying thread. Trim poly yarn post to one-eighth inch long or less. Try to make the tiny post stand at about a 45-degree angle.

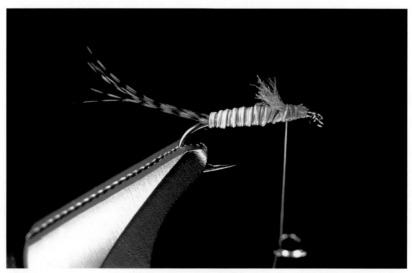

Tail, body, and poly tuft tied in and trimmed

6. Dub the thorax with only one or two turns of loosely dubbed, very fine dry-fly dubbing.

7. Whip-finish, and apply a tiny drop of head cement to the thread head only.

Tiny Bugskin Buckskin Nymph

SMALL BUCKSKIN NYMPHS

One of the most effective flies for fishing tailwaters is the Buckskin Nymph, invented by George Bodmer of Colorado Springs, Colorado. It's often the fly of the day almost anytime of year. It's quick and easy to tie in #16 through 12. Simply tie on a tail of soft brown hackle, then wrap a narrow strip of chamois around the hook, apply a whip-finish, add a small drop of head lacquer, and the fly is done.

Some major problems arise, however, when you attempt to tie this pattern in #18 through 22—sizes that are often needed. It's difficult to find chamois skins thin enough or to cut the strips narrow enough to tie a tiny Buckskin Nymph. Additional frustration comes from the fact that the narrow chamois strips required for the smaller versions pull apart very easily.

A leather product called Bugskin is stocked in many colors in many of the larger fly shops across the country. The split side has the same appearance as chamois; the other side is smooth. It's about half the thickness of chamois, has amazing tensile strength, and can be cut into narrow one-sixteenth-inch-wide strips with a thin steel straightedge and an X-Acto knife.

The only trick is to cut one side of the narrow strip at a long shallow angle similar to the shape of a long turkey biot. A 1-inch strip is long enough to tie one fly and provides a very nicely tapered body.

Hook: Any dry-fly hook, #22 through 16.

Tail: Optional. Light brown hackle fibers.

Body: Narrow strip of chamois-colored Bugskin.

Thread: Color to match Bugskin.

Head: Finish off with black thread.

1. Cover the hook shank with tying thread from the hook eye to the beginning of the hook bend.

2. Use a steel straightedge ruler and a razor blade or X-Acto knife to cut a strip of Bugskin about one-sixteenth inch wide.

3. Use your scissors to cut one end of the strip at a long shallow angle. Tie the point onto the hook at the hook bend (butt of the strip to the rear) by catching the tip with tying thread.

4. Bring the tying thread forward to hang down about one hook-eye space behind the eye, wrap the Bugskin strip forward in overlapping wraps, and tie it off one hook-eye space behind the eye.

5. Lift the remainder of the Bugskin strip and snip it off at an angle immediately behind the eye.

6. Cover the remaining butt completely, whip-finish, and apply a tiny drop of head lacquer to the thread wraps only.

BIOT MIRACLE NYMPH

Hook: Any dry-fly hook, #20 through 14.

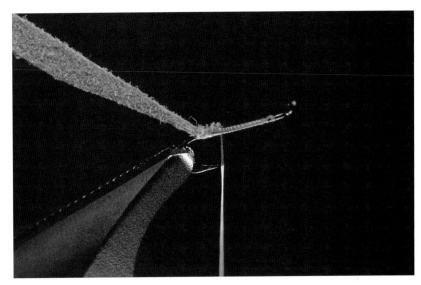

Bugskin strip tied to hook

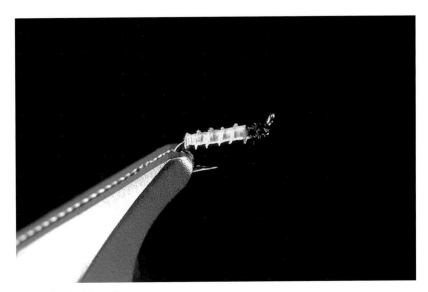

Biot Miracle Nymph

Thread: Black (underbody and head).

Body: White duck or goose biot.

Note: See chapter 14 for instructions on tying with biots.

The original pattern calls for a black thread underbody over which white floss is wrapped and ribbed with copper wire. I like the segmented appearance of the biot body better, and since biots are quite durable, I can omit the copper rib.

I list "any dry-fly hook" for the above patterns rather than the use of the heavier wire nymph hooks for three reasons:

1. The fine-wire hook is less noticeable.
2. I can grease the fly and float it in the surface film.
3. I want these tiny flies to drift beneath the surface with all the delicacy of the naturals when I fish them wet.

I add a small piece of lead putty substitute to the tippet about 14 to 16 inches above the fly when I want it to go deeper. If regulations won't allow this on your favorite stream, you'll have to use the heavier wire nymph hooks, or add a few turns of fine lead wire to the hook shank before you tie the fly. I don't like either of these options, because the added weight seems to make the fly drift unnaturally in the water.

Fishing these tiny flies is great fun. If you're like me, you'll lose a lot of them, hopefully some to fish. That's why I like to keep them as simple as possible. It doesn't hurt so much when I lose one in the bushes behind me.

TINY SOFT-HACKLE FLIES

We've known for quite some time that soft-hackle wet flies are very effective almost anytime we go fly fishing. Most of the soft-hackle wet flies I've seen in fly shops and in some of my friends' fly boxes are no smaller than #14 because in nearly every case the fly recipe calls for one or two turns of partridge hackle. Size 16 and smaller partridge hackle is very difficult to come by, so tyers limit themselves to the size of fly they can tie by the size of the hackle that is available.

No law states that you must use partridge hackle to tie soft-hackle flies. Look around in your local fly shop or browse the Web, and you'll be able to find some barred hen necks and backs with feathers down to #16 and 18 that are nicely webbed right out to the hackle tips. These feathers make wonderful soft-hackle collars and are available in the right colors. Another alternative would be to purchase a light grizzly hen neck and dye it to a light shade of brown or tan. If you can't find a hen neck with feathers whose fibers are short enough to hackle a #18 or 20 wet fly, follow the tying instructions below.

OLIVE QUILL SOFT-HACKLE EMERGER

This fly is a variation of Roy Palm's Biot Emerger in which he uses a dyed goose biot for the body and wraps one or two turns of a small dun hen hackle for the collar. Small (#20, 22, and 24) hen neck hackle is difficult to find, quite wispy, and fragile to work with. I prefer to use hen neck or back segments to eliminate these shortcomings.

I've tied flies down to #20 and 22 with this method. When treated with a good dry-fly floatant, they make wonderful BWO emergers.

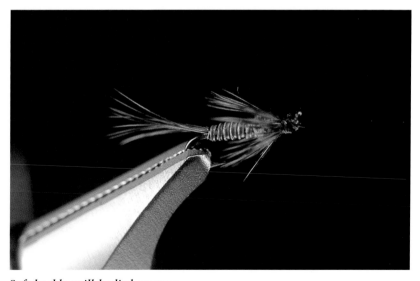

Soft-hackle quill-bodied emerger

Hook: Your favorite dry-fly hook, #18 through 22.

Thread: Olive 6/0.

Tail: Four or five fibers of mottled hen back.

Body: Medium olive quill.

Thorax: Fine medium dun dubbing.

Hackle: Segment of mottled brown hen back feather, spun in wet-fly-style.

1. Start the thread at midshank and wrap to the beginning of the hook bend.

2. Select a densely webbed and prominently mottled feather from near the middle of the hen back (save the larger butt feathers for larger flies). Strip the fluffy marabou fibers from the base.

Densely webbed and prominently marked hen back feather with fluff stripped off

3. Even the hackle tips by stroking the hackle fibers toward the butt of the feather to stand at a 90-degree angle to the stem. Clip or pull four or five fibers from the base and tie them onto the hook for the tail, which should be equal in length to the entire hook. Lash the bundle to within three hook-eye lengths of

the eye, lift the butts, and clip them off. Leave the thread hanging here.

Tail tied in, butts clipped and thread hanging

4. Select one medium olive quill and clip off the tip at a point where its diameter is equal to that of the tailing, hook, and thread.

5. Lay the quill on the hook, clipped tip lined up with the clipped tailing butts (quill butt to the rear); lash it to the hook all the way to the hook bend. Bring the thread back forward to one hook-gap space behind the eye.

6. Wrap the quill forward with tightly nested wraps to within one hook-gap space of the eye, tie it down with thread, clip off the butt on top of the hook, and smooth the clipped quill butt with tying thread.

7. Apply a tiny amount of fine medium dun dubbing to the tying thread. With only two turns of dubbing, form a small thorax and abrupt shoulder on top of the quill body shoulder. Leave the remainder of the hook shank bare to the eye.

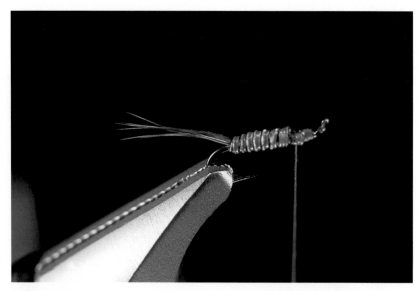

Body complete

Thorax applied

8. Stroke the hen hackle fibers toward the butt of the feather to
    make the tips even. Grasp a one-quarter-inch-wide segment
    and remove it from the hackle stem by *pulling the stem away*

from the segment. If you try to pull the segment from the stem, you'll misalign all the tips.

Pulling stem from segment

9. Align the tips even with the end of the hook bend and transfer the clump to your left hand. Hold the segment (tips to the rear) slightly to the far side of the hook to touch the shoulder, and take one loose turn of tying thread over the segment *immediately* in front of the shoulder.

10. Slowly tighten the thread to distribute the fibers completely around the hook. You may have to encourage the last few fibers to spread by pressing on them with your right-hand thumbnail.

11. You can add a smaller segment to fill in any gaps that you can't force into place with your thumbnail.

12. Take three or four more turns of thread to lock the collar in place, clip off the butts as close as possible to the hook, whip-finish, and apply a tiny drop of head lacquer to the thread head only. Some of the heavily webbed fibers may appear to be stuck together. Simply "ping" the hook eye and the vibration will separate them.

Segment in place with one loose turn of thread

Collar spread evenly

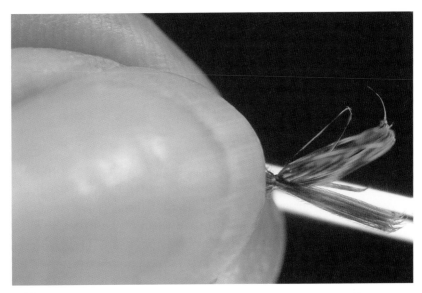

Adding segment

HACKLE COLOR AND HEN NECKS

Fishing the Trico spinner fall has been a popular event for many years. Dozens of articles on it have appeared in all the fly-fishing magazines. Each article is accompanied by a photo or two of the natural Trico spinners with black legs. I think many fly tyers assume that the duns have black legs as well, and that's the way they're tied. Next time you're fishing a Trico hatch without much success, though, take a moment to observe the legs of the naturals. I'd be willing to bet that your imitation has black hackle, and that the natural has cream-colored legs. I've yet to see a dun with black legs, yet all the spinners' legs are black. Bob Miller's book *Tricos,* published by Rod Crafters Press in 1997, is an excellent source for some good instruction in tying Trico duns and spinners. It's interesting to note that he advises using light dun hackle for both the male and female dun patterns.

Take a moment next time you're fishing a BWO hatch to catch a few naturals and look at the color of their legs. Chances are, they'll have creamy-colored legs without a hint of gray. Not all small

BWOs have gray legs, yet most tyers will hackle all sizes of BWOs with some shade of medium dun hackle. Catch some emerging black midges this winter and notice the color of their legs. Once again, they're light cream colored, not black. All the adult midges I've netted have black legs, but not the emerger, which is often the most important phase of the hatch. Yet all the midge emerger patterns have black hackle.

I have no idea why some small dry flies are traditionally tied with a hackle color that doesn't match the natural insect's legs, yet great effort is made to exactly match hackle to the leg color on some other larger flies such as the Hendrickson or Quill Gordon. Tradition rules in the world of fly fishing and fly tying. I believe that a great deal of it is based on assumptions. There seems to be a belief that since the legs are longer on a larger fly, it's more important to attempt to match the color. The legs on a smaller fly are just as long, proportionally, as they are on a large fly.

Some people have the opinion that hackle color usually doesn't matter very much. After all, we've all been catching trout on black-hackle Trico duns and midge emergers for years, and our gray-hackle Baetis duns have been working quite well for us. But there are times when we don't get so much as a refusal rise. My question is, "Where have we been fishing them?" Usually it's on open water, in current creases, and near the stream bank—all places we look to for rising fish. But what about the skinny water beneath overhanging bushes, or a tree-lined stream bank that casts dark shadows over deep holes? These are two places where it's more difficult to spot rising fish—and which are therefore overlooked. These are areas where bigger trout hang out, and more importantly, where light colors are contrasted against a darker background. Try the following experiment: Pick a medium dun and a cream hackle feather, go outside, hold them over your head, and look up at them with the open sky as the background. You'll notice that the dun hackle appears to be darker than you thought it would be, and the cream hackle isn't as visible as the gray. Now stand under a heavily leafed tree and repeat the experiment. In the shade, your cream hackle almost seems to light up, while much of the color of the gray hackle is lost. The prominence of each color is reversed in opposite lighting situations. We look *down* at a fly, a *trout* looks *up!* Your imitation will be seen by the trout either against an open-sky background or a dark shade background. Why would we think that one pattern will work well in all situations, and if not, which color do you want the trout to see?

A long-standing assumption is that dry flies must be hackled with stiff dry-fly hackle. If that's so, why are the No Hackles, Comparaduns, and Hen Wing Spinner patterns so effective? Granted, these three patterns were designed to be fished in relatively smooth water, where stiff hackle fibers aren't required to keep the fly suspended on the surface. But what about the absence of legs? Mayflies have legs, but only six of them, and they're not as thin as spider silk.

Stiff, expensive hackle simply isn't needed on small flies fished in skinny water or on glass-smooth runs near shady banks. In fact, hackling flies in the traditional manner for these situations may inhibit success. I've been hackling flies for this kind of fishing with only two turns of hen hackle for the past four or five years. Some of my #18 and smaller Baetis are hackled with two turns of cream hen hackle, as are all of my Trico Duns and Black Midge Emergers. I clip the hackle flush with the bottom of the thorax on these flies. Flotation isn't a problem due to today's modern dry-fly dressings. I use stripped and dyed rooster neck hackle quills for the bodies, which float the hook without any dry-fly dressing. The hen hackle fibers are a little thicker—which I think more accurately matches the diameter of the insects' legs—and since the fibers of a hen hackle are softer, there's some movement. I've noticed that many insects' legs move a little as they struggle for balance while drifting downstream. In consideration of these observations, I offer the following patterns, which have made my experiences fishing skinny water much more successful and enjoyable.

OLIVE QUILL BAETIS DUN, CREAM SOFT HACKLE (CSH)

Hook: Your favorite dry-fly hook, #20 through 24.

Thread: Light green 8/0.

Tail: Medium dun spade hackle fibers, length to equal hook length.

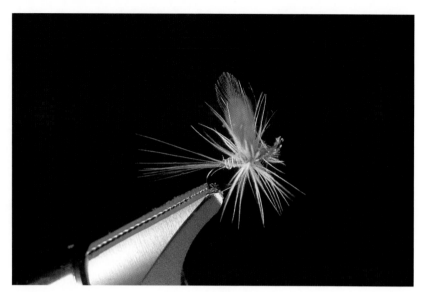

Olive Quill Baetis, CSH: Cream Soft Hackle

Body: One stripped and light green dyed rooster neck hackle quill.

Wings: Pair of medium dun hen hackle tips.

Hackle: Two turns of light ginger or cream hen hackle.

1. Attach the tying thread at midshank and wrap to the beginning of the bend, taking two turns of thread on top of the last turn of thread to create a tiny thread bump.

2. Clip five or six spade hackle fibers and tie them onto the hook immediately in front of the tiny thread bump to cock the tails up slightly. Lash the tailing butts to the hook shank to within three hook-eye spaces of the hook eye, lift the butts, and clip them off. This spot will become the shoulder of the body.

3. Select one stripped and light green dyed rooster neck hackle quill and clip off the tip at a point where the diameter of the remaining quill will be equal to the diameter of the hook, tailing butts, and thread. Place the clipped end of the quill on the hook

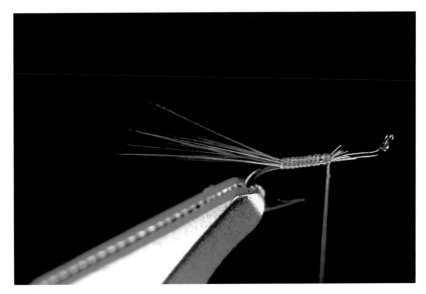

Tailing tied on

to be lined up with the clipped tailing butts and lash it to the hook by wrapping the tying thread toward the hook bend.

Quill tied on

4. Bring the tying thread forward to the shoulder and wrap the quill forward in tightly nested wraps. Tie down the quill butt on top of the hook and clip off the excess. Cover the clipped butt with tying thread until it's smooth.

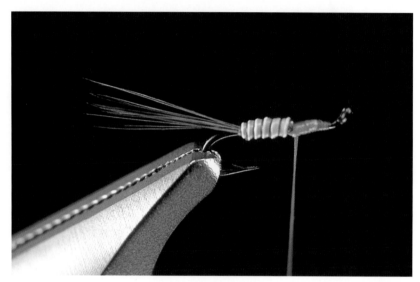

Body wrapped, trimmed, smoothed with thread

5. Select two medium dun hen hackle tips, whose width should equal the hook gap. Measure them to be as long as the entire hook plus one hook-eye space and clip off the butts. Place the wings on the hook (tips to the rear), and tie them on the hook immediately in front of the shoulder. Figure-eight the tying thread through the wings to separate, leaving the tying thread hanging immediately in front of the wings.

6. Select one light ginger or cream hen hackle feather from near the tip of the neck. The hackle fiber length should be one and a half times the hook-gap distance.

7. Trim the maraboulike fibers from near the butt of the feather and tie the butt to the hook immediately in front of the wings, dull-side up.

Wings tied on

Tiny Cream Soft Hackle, trimmed

8. Attach your hackle pliers to the tip of the feather and make the first turn of hackle straight away from you down in front of the far wing and under the hook to come around behind the wings.

Hackle tied on

The hackle feather should twist, making the hackle fibers point to the rear of the fly. Continue wrapping the hackle by bringing the feather down on the far side of the hook and forward under the hook to come up around in front of the wings. The feather will twist again, causing the hackle fibers to lean forward. Take one complete turn of hackle in front of the wings, tie down the tip, and clip away the excess.

9. Whip-finish, trim all the hackle from the bottom of the fly even with the thorax area, and apply a tiny drop of head lacquer to the head.

TRICO QUILL DUN, CREAM SOFT HACKLE (CSH)

Hook: Your favorite dry-fly hook, #18 through 22.

Thread: Cream 8/0.

Tail: Pale dun spade hackle fibers.

Body: Stripped and pale green or dark green dyed rooster neck hackle. Note: Some Tricos have a pale green body, some a dark green. If you opt to tie

First twist

Second twist

Trico Quill Dun, CSH

the dark green version, you should substitute light medium dun hen hackle for both the wings and hackle, and switch to olive thread to tie in the hackle and whip-finish.

Thorax: One or two turns of fine dry-fly charcoal or black dubbing, to be applied over the shoulder of the quill body.

Wings: Pair of white hen hackle tips, or light dun for the dark green version.

Hackle: Two turns of light ginger or cream hen hackle, or light medium dun for the dark green version.

BLACK MIDGE EMERGER, CREAM SOFT HACKLE (CSH)

Hook: Your favorite dry-fly hook, #16 through 22.

Thread: Black 8/0 for tail and abdomen, cream for tying in hackle.

Tail: Five or six wood duck flank feather fibers or dyed mallard, length to equal hook shank.

Body: One stripped and black-dyed rooster neck hackle quill.

Wing: Segment of waffle-imprinted clear plastic strip. Use Glad Lock bags— the kind that says, "Yellow and Blue makes Green." There is a waffle imprint on either side of the closure strip that makes wonderful midge wings. Width should equal the hook-gap space.

Hackle: Two turns of light ginger or cream hen hackle.

Black Midge Emerger, CSH

1. Attach the thread to the hook at midshank and wrap to the beginning of the hook bend.

2. Select a wood duck or dyed mallard flank feather with stiff fibers and clip off only five or six fibers. Line them up on top of the hook with the tips extending beyond the hook bend by the length of one hook shank. Wrap the butts forward to within three hook-eye spaces of the hook eye, lift the butts, and trim them off. This will be the shoulder of the fly.

3. Select a stripped and black-dyed rooster neck hackle quill. Clip off the tip at a point where the remaining quill tip diameter will match the diameter of the hook, thread, and tailing butts.

4. Lash the quill to the hook with the butt to the rear and the clipped tip even with the clipped tailing butts. Wrap the thread down to the hook bend, bring the thread forward to the shoulder, and wrap the quill forward in tightly nested wraps to the shoulder. Tie down the butt with several turns of tight thread, lift the butt, and clip it off. Smooth the butt with several turns of thread.

5. Cut a strip of waffle plastic as wide as the hook gap. Clip one end to an arrow shape and tie in the point of the arrow parallel to the hook shank on top of the shoulder, and slightly to the tyer's side of the hook. Thread torque will slide it to the top of the hook. Be certain that the arrow point is tied in on top of the shoulder, not in front. This will keep the wing lying flat against the top of the quill body.

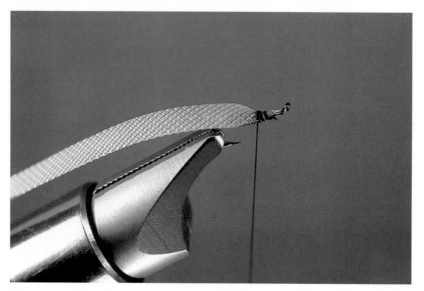

Wing strip on shoulder

6. Use your right-hand thumb and forefinger to fold a crease in the wing parallel to the hook shank. Clip the butt of the wing even with the end of the bend and trim off the corners of the wing butt.

7. Select one light ginger or cream hen hackle from near the tip of the neck. The hackle fiber length should be one and a half times the hook gap.

8. Change to cream thread. Strip away all the marabou fibers from the base of the feather, and tie the butt of the hackle shiny-side down onto the hook immediately in front of the shoulder of the body.

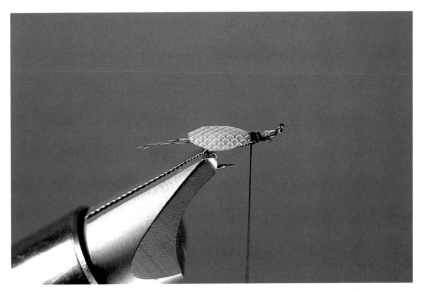

Folded and trimmed wing strip

9. Attach your hackle pliers to the tip of the hackle and take only two turns of hackle toward the hook eye. Tie off the tip, clip the excess, and whip-finish. Clip the hackle from the bottom of the fly and add a tiny drop of head lacquer.

FLOATING NYMPHS

I am a devout dry-fly fisherman. I'll fish nymphs if there are no trout rising within sight, but all it takes is for me to see one or two rises from a single trout and I'll happily spend the greater part of a day trying to figure out what it was that brought that fish to the surface.

A few years ago, I was camped on the banks of Colorado's Frying Pan River hoping to catch the fall Baetis hatch. The first day was easy—the trout wanted a #18 Olive Quill Dun. On the second day, they preferred the parachute version. The third day it took me a little longer to figure out that what they wanted was the spinner. On the fourth day, they wouldn't look at anything but a floating emerger, and on the fifth (and my last) day, I spent most of my time changing flies. I finally waded into the feeding lane and netted the water with my little aquarium net. Much to my surprise, floating nymphs (not emergers!) far outnumbered duns, spinners, and emergers. There were many duns on the water each day, but for some reason, the trout changed their preference from day to day.

I waded back to my casting position and searched my nymph box for a #18 Baetis Nymph with a dark wing case pad. I had only three. I tied one to my 6X tippet and thoroughly greased it with a paste floatant. By the time I had accomplished that, the trout were feeding at the surface again. I hooked and landed a fish on my first lightly presented cast. A very fat 16-inch rainbow rose and ate my floating nymph with all the confidence he had shown toward the naturals. I fished the greased floating nymph all morning and caught more than my share of fish, and I learned another lesson from the trout: Don't assume anything.

I fish unweighted and greased mayfly nymphs because I want the fly to float slightly above the stream bottom with my lead substitute putty bouncing along on the rocks 14 to 16 inches up on the tippet. I lose far fewer flies this way, and I believe I'm getting more strikes. Lately I've been tying all my mayfly nymphs as if I were going to fish them as dry flies. I can fish them at any level in the water column by adding varying amounts of lead substitute putty to the tippet. You can literally tie any mayfly nymph as a floating nymph simply by varying the color of the tailing and dubbing for the body and thorax.

FLOATING HARE'S EAR NYMPH

Hook:	Dry fly, #18 through 14.
Thread:	6/0, lighter than dubbing (tan for Hare's Ear and light olive for BWO).
Tailing and Underbody:	Twelve to eighteen (depending on hook size) dark, hollow elk-hair fibers.
Overbody:	Thinly and tightly applied dubbing (hare's-ear color for Hare's Ear and light olive for BWO).
Ribbing:	6/0 thread, darker than dubbing (brown for Hare's Ear and olive for BWO).
Wing Case:	Dark gray goose segment.
Thorax:	Loosely dubbed, slightly darker than abdomen.

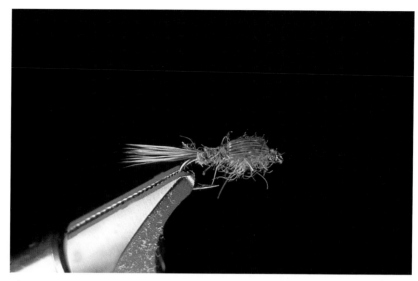

Floating Hare's Ear Nymph

Floating BWO Nymph

Tail and underbody:

1. Stack the elk-hair tips to even and tie them in at the hook bend to extend beyond the bend by one hook-gap length.

2. Spiral-wrap the tying thread over the elk forward to within two hook-eye distances of the hook eye. Leave the elk pointing forward over the eye.

3. Bring the thread back toward the bend in one open wrap *underneath* the hook, to hang down one hook-gap space behind the eye. This is the thorax area.

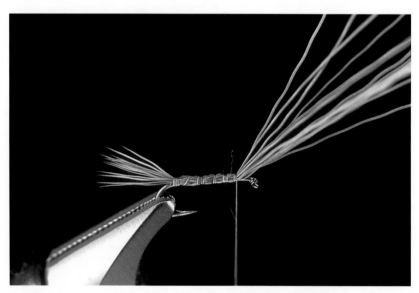

First layer of elk hair

4. Lift the elk, fold it back over the top of the hook, and tie down with only two turns of tying thread. You have now created a double layer of elk on top of the hook at the thorax area.

5. Bring the thread back to the front of the thorax area in one open wrap *beneath* the hook, and fold the hair forward again. Tie the hair down with two turns of tying thread.

Second layer at thorax

6. Bring the thread back toward the rear of the thorax area in one open wrap below the hook, tie in the ribbing if you choose to have it, and continue wrapping in open spirals to the rear of the abdomen. Clip off the hair butts. You have created a three-layer elk-hair thorax area.

   Overbody:

7. Apply a thin layer of tight dubbing to the tying thread and wrap forward to create the abdomen. Wrap the dubbing to the rear of the thorax, then wrap the ribbing in open spirals forward to the rear of the thorax, tie off, and trim away the tag end.

   Wing case:

8. Tie in a dark gray segment of goose quill by its butt immediately behind the thorax with the segment tip pointing to the rear. The width of the segment should be equal to the hook-gap space.

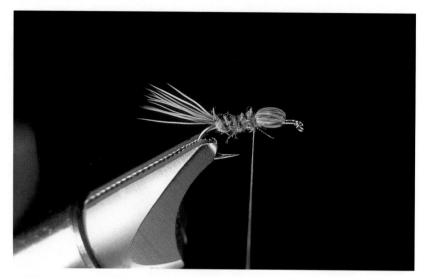

Dubbed abdomen and ribbing

Thorax:

9. Dub a loose thorax area, pull the goose segment forward over the top, tie down, clip off the excess tip of the goose quill, and apply a whip-finish. Tease out the thorax dubbing with a dubbing teaser and apply a drop of head lacquer on the head thread wraps only. Try to avoid getting any head lacquer on the goose segment, because it will prevent your dry-fly floatant from penetrating into it.

I prefer tying the elk hair in as an underbody rather than over the top as a shellback because trouts' teeth can't cut it apart. The fly has built-in flotation without the use of any synthetic material. I'll admit this is not a high-visibility floating nymph, but I figure the trout will show me where it is when they eat it. Besides, I have yet to see a natural with a chunk of bright neon yellow stuff on its back.

QUILL-BODIED NYMPHS

The Pheasant Tail Nymph and the Baetis Nymph occupy more space in my nymph box than any other nymph patterns. Tying them with the option of fishing them as dry flies has enlarged that space considerably. However, I don't tie them with an elk-hair underbody. My latest version is to make the bodies of both nymphs from stripped and dyed rooster neck hackle quills. An underbody of elk hair creates too much bulk on these slender-bodied nymphs. They lose their gill-like appearance of a dubbed or pheasant tail fiber abdomen, but the loosely dubbed thorax area seems to make up for it.

All flies tied with quill bodies are naturally buoyant and can be fished on the surface all day if a good-quality fly floatant has been applied. The waterproofed quill-bodied nymph will float on the surface film or can be fished at any depth in the water column by adding a little lead substitute putty 14 to 16 inches up on the leader tippet.

QUILL-BODIED PHEASANT TAIL NYMPH

Hook: Any appropriate size dry-fly hook.

Thread: Black or dark brown 6/0 or 8/0.

Tail: Three brown pheasant tail fibers.

Body: One or two stripped and dark tan dyed rooster neck hackle quills.

Wing Pad: Black goose segment, width to equal hook gap.

Thorax: Medium brown hare's-ear dubbing, loosely applied.

1. Start the thread on the hook at midshank and cover the hook shank toward the rear. Stop at the beginning of the bend.

2. Select three brown pheasant tail fibers and tie them onto the hook with the tips extending beyond the bend by one hook-gap space. Wrap tying thread over the tailing butts to within three hook-eye spaces of the hook eye. Lift the butts and clip them off.

3. Select one or two dark tan hackle quills (one for #18 and smaller; two for #16 and larger). Clip off the tips at a point where the quill diameter is equal to the diameter of the hook, tailing butts, and thread.

4. Lay the clipped tip parallel to the hook shank with the tip even with the clipped tailing butts and wrap with tying thread toward the hook bend. Do not wrap thread all the way to the tailing, or the first turn of the quill will push the tailing out of

Quill-bodied Pheasant Tail Nymph and Baetis Nymph

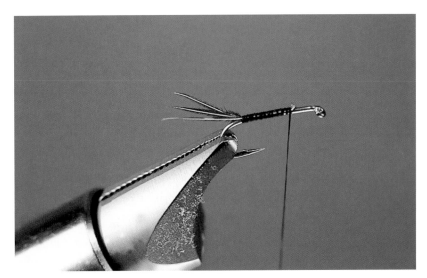

Tail fibers tied on

position. Wrap the single quill forward in tightly nested wraps, tie down the butt three hook-eye spaces behind the hook eye with five or six tight turns of tying thread, lift the butt, and trim it off. Cover the trimmed quill butt with tying thread.

Quill tied onto hook

5. You'll need to use two quills for a #16 or larger fly to get the body diameter a little larger. Select two quills, one of which will be twice the diameter of the other. Trim the tips as instructed above and place them on the hook shank with the thinner quill on the far side of the hook shank and the thicker one on the tyer's side. Wrap them forward with the thinner quill as the leader and the thicker quill as the follower to cover the leader. The thinner quill is merely an underbody.

6. Tie the butt end of a goose segment on top the quill body one hook-gap space behind the eye, with the tip pointing to the rear.

7. Dub a loose thorax that will be at least twice the diameter of the body. Begin wrapping the dubbing one hook-eye space behind the eye, and continue wrapping to the rear. Try to finish the dubbing with the tying thread at the rear of the thorax. Bring the tying thread over the top of the thorax and forward in the same turn of thread. This will flatten the top of the thorax and make it a lot easier to fold the goose segment forward.

Detail of thread at rear of thorax being brought forward on top

8. Pull the goose segment forward over the top of the thorax and tie down with very firm turns of tying thread immediately behind the hook eye. Lift the segment tip and carefully trim it as close to the thread wraps as possible.

9. Apply a whip-finish knot and trim the thread.

10. Use a dubbing teaser to tease out a generous amount of thorax dubbing.

11. Apply a small drop of head lacquer to the thread head only.

QUILL BODY BAETIS NYMPH

Hook:	Any appropriate size dry-fly hook.
Thread:	Danville's 6/0 olive.
Tail:	Small clump of dark medium dun spade hackle fibers.
Body:	One or two stripped and medium dark green dyed rooster hackle quills.
Wing Pad:	Dark dun goose quill segment, width to equal hook-gap space.
Thorax:	Olive hare's mask, applied loosely.

1. Clip a three-sixteenths-inch or slightly smaller segment of hackle fibers for the tailing and follow the tying instructions listed above for tying the Quill-Bodied Pheasant Tail Nymph.

I can't imagine there is a trout in any catch-and-release water in North America that hasn't been hooked at least once with a Pheasant Tail or Baetis Nymph. These two quill-bodied nymphs will give them something new to consider. For me, it's often been the difference between no fish and some fish.

LITTLE YELLOW CRANE FLY

The little yellow crane fly is often mistaken for a small sulphur dun. Both hatches have become rather important on the Frying Pan River because they occur at almost the same time in the mid- to late summer. In flight, the little yellow crane fly trails its long curving legs behind its body. At first glance, it looks much like a sulphur dun, tail and all.

Roy Palm invented a parachute version with a thin yellow dubbed body, white poly wing post, white delta-shaped hen hackle tip wings, and white oversized parachute hackle on a #18 hook. It's a marvelous imitation of the natural, but a real pain to tie. The natural insect's body is a true #18, but like all crane flies, it has very long legs that are best imitated using #2 white spade hackle. The wings are white as well and are about a #16 or 14. It's a challenge to get all that on such a small hook in such a way that it looks like an insect. It can be done, and the trout seem to think it's the real thing. Still, I have wondered if the extra effort was needed.

Roy's Parachute Yellow Crane Fly

My answer came one afternoon when only a few trout were rising in a current crease along the side of a long slow run, and they wouldn't accept anything but Roy's Yellow Crane Fly. Naturally, I lost my last fly high up in the bushes behind me when I missed a strike. As I waded across the stream back to camp, I noticed that a few of the naturals on the water were crumpled and stuck in the surface film. Tangled legs and twisted wings gave them the appearance of little yellow wet flies floating on the surface. "Why not?" I thought, and rushed back to camp to tie a few flies that would look like they'd been chewed up and spit out. It was just the fly the trout wanted to see, and I landed another half dozen trout before the feeding ended.

A. K.'s Crippled Yellow Crane Fly

This is another example of why it's important to carry more than one imitation of the same insect. Aquatic insect emergence doesn't always occur perfectly. There will always be some insects that are either clumsy and fall over, or have some imperfection in their development, making them vulnerable to the predators below. Trout are very efficient and will generally key in on easy prey, no matter what's hatching.

ROY'S PARACHUTE YELLOW CRANE FLY

Hook: Your favorite dry-fly hook, #18 through 20.

Thread: Yellow 6/0 or 8/0.

Tail: None.

Wing Post: White poly yarn, clipped short.

Body: Fine pale yellow dry-fly dubbing.

Wings: Pair of white hen hackle tips, tied delta-wing-style.

Hackle: Size 2 white rooster spade hackle, two turns.

1. Attach a small-diameter white poly yarn segment two hook-eye spaces behind the hook eye. Stand the post up, wrap the base of the post with tying thread, and apply a small drop of head lacquer.

2. Dub a very tight, thin body up to the post.

3. Attach one horizontal wing at a time immediately in front of the body to each side of the hook. The shoulder of the body will hold the wings in a delta configuration.

4. Attach the hackle by its butt immediately in front of the wing post and make two turns of hackle around the base of the wing post parachute-style.

5. Whip-finish and apply a small drop of head lacquer to both the hackle collar and the thread head.

6. Trim the wing post to one-eighth inch high.

A. K.'S CRIPPLED YELLOW CRANE FLY

Hook: Your favorite dry-fly hook, #18 through 20.

Thread: Yellow 6/0 or 8/0.

Tail: None.

Body: Fine pale yellow dry-fly dubbing.

Hackle: Size 2 soft white hen hackle, two turns.

1. Dub a firm, slender body to within two hook-eye spaces of the hook eye.

2. Tie in a #2 white hen hackle wet-fly-style, with the fibers curving to the rear. Take two turns and tie off.

3. Whip-finish and apply a tiny drop of head lacquer to the thread
    head.

Roy's parachute version can be fished as you would any dry fly.
My crippled version is best fished by casting across and slightly
downstream, as you would when fishing wet flies. Even though you
should apply a good dry-fly paste floatant and fish the fly as you
would a dry fly, allow the fly to get drowned at the end of the drift.
Trout will often take the fly just under the surface as it swings across
the current. Keep your rod tip up while the fly is dry. When the fly
goes beneath the surface, move your rod tip down near the surface
and keep it at a 90-degree angle to your fly line to allow the tip to
absorb the shock of a strike on a tight line.

ELEVEN

Spinning Deer Hair on Small Hooks

*

The first fly that comes to my mind when someone mentions clipped deer-hair-bodied dry flies is the Goddard Caddis. I've tied hundreds of dozens of these "G. D." Caddis and have worked out a few tricks that make tying them a little easier. The result is a rather pretty little fly.

There are three important considerations to be made before tying a small (#12 to 16) clipped spun deer-hair-bodied dry fly. The first is the selection of the deer hair. Contrary to bass bug tying, where you should use coarse, hollow hair, here you should choose finer hollow hair. Since this hair is a little softer, you can use 6/0 tying thread without having to worry about the fine thread cutting through the hair as you spin it onto the hook. This finer, softer hair can be found farther down on the deer's side.

The second most important thing is to use small amounts of hair in each bundle you tie on the hook. The amount of hair should never exceed the diameter of a standard wooden kitchen match.

Using small bundles of hair will allow you to tightly pack more bundles of hair onto the hook. The final result will be a smooth, dense body.

Coarse and fine deer hair

Third, you should learn how to use a razor blade when trimming the body to shape. I prefer a single-edge blade such as Gem simply because there's less of a chance of cutting myself. Trimming with a razor blade will result in a much cleaner cut in less time.

GODDARD CADDIS

Hook:	Your favorite dry-fly hook, #12 through 16.
Thread:	Yellow or beige 6/0, prewaxed.
Body:	Spun light tan or beige natural deer hair. Bleached deer hair tends to be a little brittle; avoid using it when spinning deer-hair bodies.
Antennas:	Two hand-stripped ginger hackle quills.
Hackle:	Stiff ginger neck or saddle.

Goddard Caddis

1. Start the thread on the hook at the bend and make seven or eight very tight turns on top of each other. Leave the rest of the hook shank bare. Clip off the tag and apply a tiny drop of Zap-A-Gap or superglue and wait for it to dry. This is a crucial first step in that the glued thread wraps will prevent the first bundle of hair from sliding down into the hook bend when you pack on the second and third bundles.

2. Select a small clump of fine, hollow deer hair and clip the tips back to leave a bundle that's only about one-half inch long.

3. Place the bundle (butts to the rear!) parallel to the top of the hook at midshank and take two loose turns of tying thread over it. Begin to tighten the thread slightly as you continue to make a third turn. Release your grip on the bundle as soon as you notice the deer hair beginning to flare, and continue wrapping a fourth turn in the same place. If you're having a good day, the hair bundle will spin completely around the hook. Use your right-hand thumb and forefinger to slide the bundle

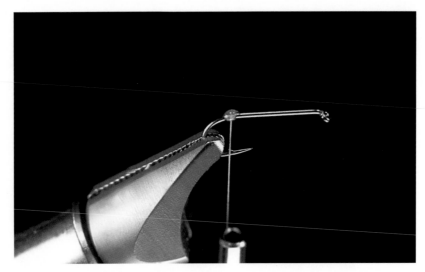

Thread bump with glue

tightly against the thread bump. Bring the tying thread forward through the clump and make two turns in front of the
clump to anchor it in place. Some of the hair may get hung up
on the hook point. Simply use your dubbing needle to free it.
You may have to use your right forefinger and thumb to adjust
the bundle by twisting it slightly from side to side to distribute
the hair evenly around the hook.

4. Place the thumbnail of your left hand against the thread bump,
    then fold and compress the hair clump to the rear as much as
    you can with your right-hand thumb and forefinger.

5. Repeat with a second small bundle of hair tied in immediately
    in front of the first. Use a hair packer to compress the clump
    tightly against the first.

6. Spin a third clump if you have enough hook-shank space re-
    maining. Save at least a hook-gap space behind the eye for an-
    tennas and hackle collar. Cover the remaining hook shank
    with thread and leave the bobbin hanging just behind the hook
    eye.

First hair clump spun and compressed

Spun body

7. Invert the fly and use a razor blade to trim off the bottom of the fly first. Use the bottom edge of the hook eye as a blade guide and slice toward the hook bend. Be very careful that you

don't get too close to the hook shank, or you'll cut through the thread wraps that anchor the deer hair. Also be aware that you must allow as much hook-gap space as you can.

First cut with razor blade

8. Turn the fly right-side up, place the blade close to the hook shank at the front of the body, and slice from near the hook shank to the rear, allowing the hair near the butt of the fly to be about as long as the hook-gap width, creating one side of a 50- to 60-degree triangle. Don't worry about straggling hair fibers at the rear; we'll deal with them later.

9. Repeat another identical cut to the other side of the body. You should now have a three-sided, elongated-triangle-shaped body.

10. Use a straight-blade scissors to square up the rear of the body.

11. Select two 2- to 3-inch-long ginger hackle feathers and hand-strip all the hackle fibers from both sides of the quill.

First side cut

Completed body shaped

Squaring up the rear with scissors

12. Tie in the antennas with the dull sides up and separated in a narrow V shape. Firmly lash them down all the way to the hook eye. Bring the tying thread back to the beginning of the body.

13. Tie in the stiffest ginger saddle or neck hackle you can find and wrap it forward in tightly nested (but not overlapping) wraps to within one hook-eye space behind the eye. Tie off, trim away the tip, and take a couple of turns under the antennas to cock them up a little. Whip-finish on top of the antennas and apply a drop of head lacquer to both the thread head and the bottom of the fly's body.

14. Curl the antennas one at time by pinching the quill between your thumbnail (with the thumbnail on top of the quill) and forefinger and pulling toward the tip of the quill. Be very careful that you don't pinch too hard and pull the antenna off the hook. It's best to apply pressure in small amounts at first, to learn how much it takes to curl the quill.

Fish this fly carefully. It took a long time to tie, and it's too pretty to lose!

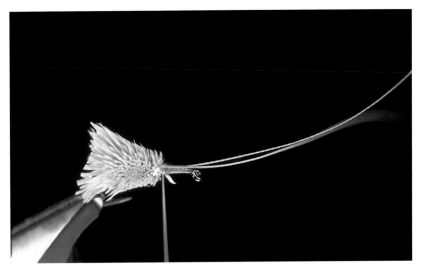

Antennas tied in

Tying a few flies that require spun deer or elk hair can literally be a painful experience. Many tyers will pull and compress the hair clump back toward the rear of the hook using their thumb and the first two fingers of their materials hand. I do it this way because it's very quick and effective for creating a flat face on a clump of deer hair before tying in the next clump. The hook point will invariably prick the pad of your third finger when you do this. It's not unusual to draw a little blood after tying only one or two flies. You can avoid the pain and bloodshed by wearing a latex Finger Tip on your third finger.

The Finger Tip by Swingline is available at most well-stocked office supply stores and was designed for use by people who handle lots of loose pages or paper money and need to be able to sort one sheet at a time. Like many other gadgets we adopt for fly-tying use, you'll have to alter the design of the original a little to make it a useful aid. The Finger Tip has dozens of tiny latex bumps all around it that cling to the deer and elk hair too much. You can deal with these by putting it on your finger and then carefully snipping them off with a sharp pair of scissors, or you can simply turn it inside out; it's smooth on the inside.

Fingertip

Wearing a Finger Tip while you tie with clumps of deer or elk hair will seem a little awkward at first, but after two or three flies, you'll be glad you took the time to get accustomed to it.

TWELVE

Quill-Bodied Sulphurs

I've been dreaming of fishing the sulphur hatch on some of the famous Pennsylvania spring creeks for more than thirty years. The spring of 1999 was my lucky year, because not only did I go, I hit the sulphur hatch in all its glory. My friends Mike Clark and John Gierach went in '98 but were almost blown out by high water from torrential rains. They fished with Walt Carpenter of bamboo-rod-making fame, and when they returned they told me that I had to go the next year. Penns Creek, Spring Creek, Big Spring Creek, and Spruce Creek were absolutely beautiful, and they'd caught some fish even in the high water. How could I refuse? Besides, it would give me an opportunity to test some Quill-Bodied Sulphur patterns I had been working on; I needed to know if the colors were right.

I started putting a few dollars away each month for nearly a year to make the trip I had always dreamed of. John and Mike picked me up on the morning of May 15, and we were off to Denver to catch a plane first to Dulles International, then back to State College, Pennsylvania, where Walt and his fishing partner Carl Roszkowski met us for the drive to the Spruce Creek Rod and Gun Club. There we were all guests of Walt's good friend Bob Budd. The only glitch in the trip involved the short flight from Dulles to State College. We were about halfway to our destination when the pilot of the little twin-engine plane informed us that we had to turn around and go back to Dulles because the passenger door wasn't properly sealed and therefore the plane couldn't be pressurized. I looked out the window and thought, "Hell, I live at an altitude (Boulder is at 5,600 feet) that's higher than we're flying. Why go back?" But we did, and finally landed at State College about two hours late. The important thing is that we got there, and so did all our gear.

The next two days are kind of a blur in my memory. John, Mike, Carl, Walt, and Bob were all catching lots of fish with a Pheasant Tail Nymph behind a Sulphur Dun. I, however, am a firm believer in catching one trout at a time and chose to fish a single dry Quill-Bodied Sulphur Dun.

We fished Spring Creek on Wednesday. I staked out a likely-looking pool below a long riffle that I figured would be productive as the afternoon wore on. I sat on the bank for two hours, watching the occasional rise as the clouds gradually gathered and blotted out the sun.

Then it began to happen. The late-afternoon sun was completely blocked by clouds and the sulphurs began to hatch. Soon the air above the stream was swarming with thousands of mayflies—and the trout began to rise. I caught six or eight 12- to 14-inch browns on a #16 Quill-Bodied Sulphur Dun fished under some low-hanging tree limbs. Then I noticed that the rise form was different, a softer take with little sound, so I tied on a #16 Pale Yellow Quill-Bodied Spinner.

My first fish on the spinner was a heavy 18-inch brown that I had to chase downstream for nearly 50 yards before I could bring it to net. I measured the fish in the net, backed the little quill-bodied fly from its lower lip, and was all set to spend some time reviving the deeply colored fish in my hands. As I aimed its head into the slight current, it gave a mighty thrust of its tail and was out of sight in the blink of an eye. I don't think I've ever fought a fish so long, so hard, and watched it dash away as though nothing had happened.

I waded back to my spot thinking I'd have to wait a while for the trout in this legendary stream to start rising again. To my surprise, there appeared to be even more fish working the surface. I cast to the far bank, where there was a rise just behind a small dead limb hanging into the water, and was immediately hanging on to the rod as a 16-inch brown tore downstream with the little #16 Quill Spinner stuck to the side of its jaw.

When I returned to my spot, the pool was quiet. My fish had plowed through the surface like a speeding porpoise. In the time it took me to light another cigar, the fish were back at the surface sipping spinners. A 14-inch fish was next, followed by a 13-incher, both of which I was able to land without leaving the pool. They were strong fish and fought tenaciously, as brown trout should.

During all this action, I noticed another fisherman slowly working his way downstream into the riffle, where he stopped and fished what little pocket water and sides were there. I thought, "I'll bet if I have to chase another fish downstream, that guy will slide right down into this pool and I'll have to give him hell about it." At that very moment all hell did break loose under a low-hanging branch where I had just placed a lucky cast. I was fast to another very strong fish that ripped downstream toward what I was beginning to think of as the landing pool. It took a little more than ten minutes to bring the fish to net; I taped it at just a bit over 18 inches.

I waded back upstream fully expecting my spot to be occupied by the young fisherman in the riffle. Much to my surprise, he hadn't moved! He was still at a very discreet distance from where I had been standing. I began casting again while thinking about that and mentally adding up the number of inches of trout I had caught on the same fly in a little more than an hour. "Five fish equaling 79 inches—hell, that's longer than I am!" I looked upstream at the young fisherman and said, "Sir, thank you for not moving down here while I fought that last fish. I appreciate the fact that you are a gentleman and understand stream etiquette. How long have you been fly fishing?" He said, "Thank you, I've only been fly fishing for about two years." I'd noticed that he had only caught one or two small fish and said, "Come on down here, you've earned this spot. And besides, I think I've had about all the fun I deserve for one evening. What fly are you using?" He showed me a little brown no-name creation. I said, "Here," snapped off my little #16 Quill Spinner, and gave it to him. "Try this, it's been working very well for me." And left.

We went back to Spring Creek the following afternoon and staked out our favorite runs and pools. The hatch was just as heavy, but for some reason the trout seemed reluctant to eat our flies or the naturals. We each caught only one or two fish.

The five of us were all back at the cars early that evening, discussing our lack of success compared to the previous evening as we derigged. At about this time the same young fisherman I had given the fly to came walking by with his girlfriend. He said, "Hey, weren't you guys here last night?" We told him that we were and he said, "Well, one of you gave me a fly and I just wanted to thank you. I caught two 20-inch browns on that fly last night." I stepped forward, shook his hand, and said, "You're welcome." It was a sweet feeling. The colors were right on!

SULPHUR QUILL DUN

   Hook: Dry fly, #14, 16, 18.
Thread: Danville's 6/0 #8, yellow.
   Tail: Medium ginger spade hackle fibers, splayed.
   Body: Stripped and lemon yellow dyed rooster neck hackle quills.
  Wings: Pale smoky dun hen hackle tips.
 Hackle: Medium ginger.

Parachute:
Everything as listed for the dun above, except use a segment of white turkey T-base for the wing post.

Sulphur Quill Dun

Sulphur Quill Parachute

Sulphur Quill Spinner

SULPHUR QUILL SPINNER

Hook: Dry fly, #14, 16, 18.
Thread: Danville's #4, pale yellow.
Tail: Light ginger spade hackle fibers, splayed.
Body: Stripped and pale yellow dyed rooster neck hackle quill.
Wings: White hen hackle tips.
Thorax: Dry-fly dubbing to match quill color.

THIRTEEN

Olive Quill Dun II and Red Quill Dun II

I'd been working on some ideas to fine-tune quill-bodied dry flies that I'd used for trout that rise slowly to the fly and counted the number of wraps in my whip-finish before refusing. My fly was the correct size, the color was nearly identical, and I'd resorted to 30 inches or more of 7X tippet. Still, there were some large old browns that would refuse my offering.

So once again, I projected some color slides of the naturals on my 4-by-6-foot screen and studied them for the hundredth time. The key words mentioned above—*color was nearly identical*—leaped out at me on the 101st viewing. Most adult mayfly bodies are prominently segmented and have a waxy appearance—which is what drove me to using quill bodies in the first place. Some have bodies that are basically light creamy green with a darker thinner segment, but some are light creamy green with a narrower cream segment. Some are tan with a narrower darker segment, but some

Melon Quill

are tan with a narrower cream segment. My Melon Quill pattern is an example of this bicolor segmentation, as shown in the photo above.

The standard Olive Quill naturally has a creamy green body with dark green segmentation, and the quills I use for my Red Quill

Olive Quill Dun II

have a nice tan color with a brown edge. The darker edge on both quills is the result of the dye being able to penetrate into the quill in the tiny holes left where the hackle fibers were during the Clorox-and-water burning process. Both the Olive and Tan Quills closely match most mayfly duns in these colors. But what about those flies with the lighter cream segmentation markings? Using the Melon Quill as a model, I came up with the following dry-fly patterns, which have been the undoing of a few smart old brown trout.

OLIVE QUILL DUN II

Hook: Mustad 94840 or Tiemco 100, #14 through 16. For #18 and smaller, I recommend either a loop eye (Tiemco 101) or a turned-up eye (Mustad 94842).

Thread: Danville's 6/0 #61 (light olive) for #18 and larger; Uni-Thread 8/0 (light cahill), for #20 and smaller.

Tail: Very stiff medium dun spade hackle fibers, length to equal entire hook.

Body: Two quills: one natural cream, the other light green dyed and half the diameter of the cream quill.

Wings: Medium dun hen hackle tips.

Hackle: Medium dun dry-fly hackle.

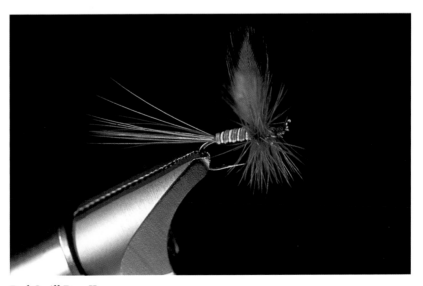

Red Quill Dun II

RED QUILL DUN II

Hook: Same as above, but in #14, 16, and 18.

Thread: Danville's 6/0, olive.

Tail: Medium dun spade hackle fibers (for dun version), length to equal entire hook.
Brown spade hackle fibers (for brown version), length to equal entire hook.

Body: Two quills: one natural cream, the other medium tan dyed and half the diameter of the cream quill.

Wings: Medium dun hen hackle tips.

Hackle: Medium dry-fly hackle for dun version.
Brown dry-fly hackle for brown version.

1. Tie in tailing and wrap butts to within one hook-gap distance of the hook eye. Lift the excess butts and clip off.

2. Select one cream quill and one dyed quill whose *combined* width is equal to the *diameter* of the hook shank, tailing, butts, and thread. You can clip off the tips to arrive at the proper width. Be certain that the cream quill will be twice the diameter of the dyed quill.

3. Place the quills on top of the hook shank with the clipped tips toward the hook eye and even with the front edge of the tailing butts. Arrange the quills so that the thicker cream quill is on the far side of the hook shank and the dyed quill is on the tyer's side of the hook, as shown in the upper photo on the facing page.

4. Grasp the quills in your left hand and move them straight away at a 90-degree angle to the hook shank. The cream quill should now be in front (lead position), and the dyed quill should now be in a position to follow the cream quill as you wrap them forward.

5. Wrap the quills forward, making sure that the dyed quill does not overlap the cream quill but follows it in tightly nested wraps, creating a narrow colored stripe or segment as you work forward.

6. Wrap the quills forward until you get to the point where the tailing butts have been clipped off. Take five or six very firm turns of tying thread and clip off the quill butts on top of the hook.

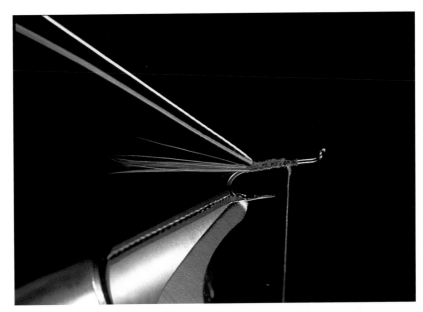

Quills tied onto hook with tailing already on

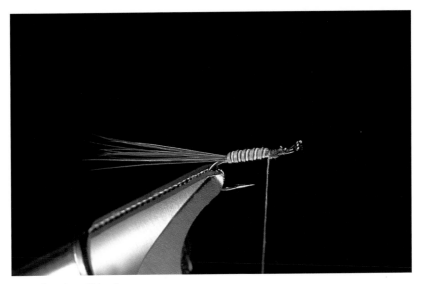

Completed quill body

Smooth the clipped quill butts with a few extra turns of tying thread.

7. Tie in the wings and divide, followed by the hackle.

There are some large old brown trout that got that way by being careful what they eat. I don't catch all of them with these new patterns, but I'm getting a few more.

FOURTEEN

Indestructible Biots
(well, almost)

———————————— ✳

Biots are those feather fibers found on the leading edge of the pointer and primary feathers of a bird's wing. Fly tyers are most interested in the biots from the domestic white goose, since these are long enough for the bodies on flies from #20 through 14. If you can get your hands on some wild turkey biots, you can probably find some that will make a body on flies from #14 through 10! Wild turkey biots are the perfect body material for large flies such as Green and Brown Drakes when you'd like to use a long-shank hook like the Tiemco 5262 or Mustad 94831. I prefer stripped and dyed rooster neck hackle quills for flies #16 and smaller, simply because the diameter of the quills is ideal to match the body segmentation of nearly all mayfly species in this size range, but I think biots are the answer for flies in #14 and larger.

I prefer wild turkey biots over goose for several reasons. I can tie nearly any mayfly adult from #14 through 10, and all those sizes can usually be found on one feather. Wild turkey biots are slightly

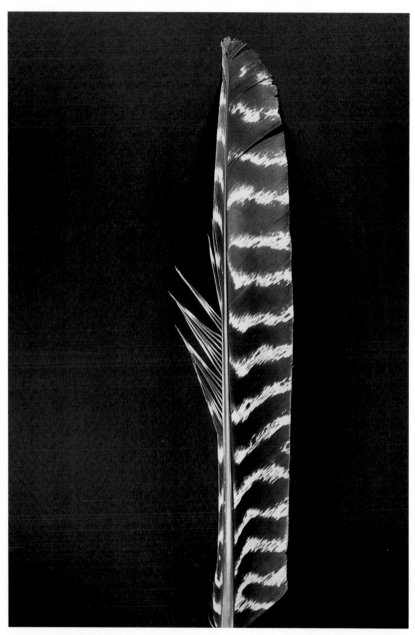

Primary turkey feather

thinner than goose biots and therefore are a little more flexible. Wild turkey biots also dye very easily and don't seem to get quite as brittle as goose biots in the dyeing process. Finally, the Velcro-like edge is often darker on a wild turkey biot, which provides a very realistic segmentation effect to the completed body, and the narrow strip on one edge of the biot has a slightly fuzzy appearance. If you don't appreciate that quality, simply wrap the biot on with the fuzzy side down.

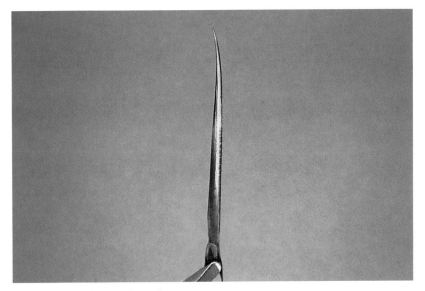

Fuzzy strip on biot and notch

How do you know if the fuzzy strip will show? Often you can see it. To be absolutely certain, look at the base of the biot where it was attached to the quill. There's a slight notch or indentation on one side of each biot near its base or wide end. This notch appears very close to the center quill, so it's important that you never clip them off. Always detach them by pulling downward toward the base of the center quill. You must do this with your thumb and forefinger by grasping one biot at a time and stripping away from the tip of the feather. If you want the Velcro-like edge to be visible after wrapping the body, make sure the notch is facing toward the hook eye after you tie it in by its tip. If you want to hide the fuzzy side, simply face the notch toward the tail of the fly.

There are a few tyers and fly fishers who don't like biot-bodied mayfly imitations because of the perceived fragile quality of the biot. I'll admit that they are thin, and a trout's tooth can cut them in just the right place. Another reason for this perceived fragility is that 6/0 (and especially 8/0) tying thread will often cut a goose biot at the tie-in point if it hasn't been tied in properly. Other causes for fragility could be that the dyeing solution used was too hot (more heat speeds up the dyeing process, but at the cost of more brittle material) or not soaking them in water long enough before use.

One answer to the trout-tooth problem has been to reverse-wrap some fine gold or silver wire over the biot body. I don't like doing this because it adds one more step to tying a fly, and I've yet to see a natural with wire wrapped around its body. I think I have a better way of reinforcing the biot body without adding any steps to the tying process. In fact, it simplifies the task. They aren't bullet-proof, but they last a lot longer. Try the following:

1. Dub a very smooth tapered underbody one hook size smaller than the hook you're tying on (a #16 body on a #14 hook). Do this for all hooks #14 and larger. Leave a space equal to two hook-eye lengths in front of the tailing material for the biot tie-down. Bring the tying thread back to the tailing tie-down. Anchor the water-soaked biot by its tip to the top of the hook shank with only one wrap of thread.

2. Grasp the butt of the biot with your left thumb and forefinger, carefully pivot the butt toward the hook eye until the biot is nearly perpendicular to the hook shank, and apply increasing tension to the first wrap of thread. This will prevent a fold on the first turn of the biot. It's this fold that often causes the biot to tear off on its first turn around the hook shank. Now tightly anchor the biot with three more turns of thread as close to the tail as possible. Let the thread hang at this point.

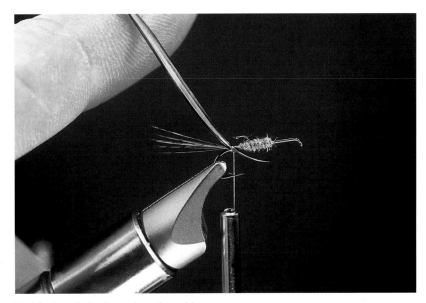

Dubbed underbody and anchored biot

Biot in perpendicular position with three turns of thread

3. Grasp the butt of the biot with your hackle pliers and take one turn of biot around the hook shank.

4. Follow with one turn of tying thread over the leading edge of the biot.

5. Take another turn of biot.

6. Continue with another turn of thread as before.

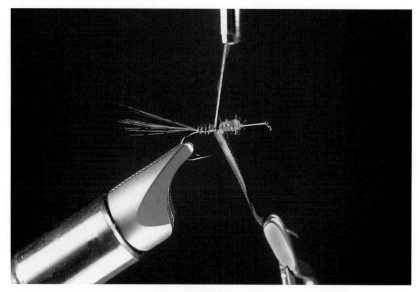

Half-completed body with thread wraps

7. Continue this procedure until you've completed the body.

8. The last wrap of thread anchors the last turn of biot!

9. Take only two or three turns of thread over the butt of the biot and clip off the butt.

Not only does this method reinforce each wrap of biot, it also prevents the last turn of biot from slipping forward over the shoulder of the underbody.

Always soak your biots in water for five or ten minutes before using. *Never* use a glycerine-and-water mixture! Water evaporates;

glycerine does not. Glycerine will soak up water as soon as the fly touches the water! The same thing is true with liquid water softeners and soaps. Besides, why not preserve the absorption qualities of the quill or biot to accept *all* the floatant when you apply it? If the tiny cells of your quills and biots are already partially filled with some other material, little of your floatant can be absorbed. It can only adhere to the surface, where it will soon wash off. It's also very important to remember that even though the water-soaked biots become very flexible, *they do not stretch.* Keep the underbody very smooth with a gradual taper.

I use monocord for tying thread on #14 hooks and larger. Wider threads have less tendency to cut the thin biots. You can always switch to 6/0 or even 8/0 after you have completed the body. Choose a thread color that closely matches the biot. I've toyed with the idea of using bright threads such as bright yellow to achieve a "glow-through" effect, but the difference is so slight that it's hardly worth the effort. It's much easier to vary the color of the biot. Once again, I strongly urge you to use body materials that are at least one shade lighter in color than the natural; they will darken after you apply your favorite waterproofing agent.

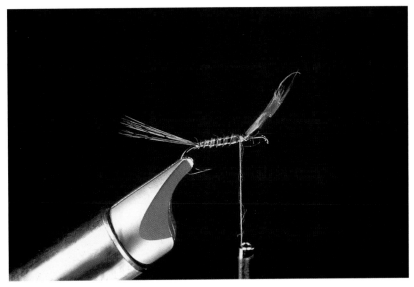

Completed fly biot body

FIFTEEN

Flavilineas

———————————— ✳

Thousands of fly fishers travel to the Rocky Mountains to fish the well-known streams during the months of July and August. When people ask what's hatching, the usual answer is "green drakes," which most folks associate with a #12 hook. But their next question should always be, "What size are the naturals?"

During any other mayfly hatch, anglers always identify the hook size *and* the name of the fly—for example, a #18 BWO, or a #16 sulphur. But large green mayflies with long gray wings aren't always green drakes. Slightly smaller flavilineas begin to hatch at about the same time that the larger green drakes are tapering off, and the two insects are often difficult to tell apart when they're flying.

I no longer ask what's hatching unless I'm fishing with someone I know very well. I once asked John Gierach what he'd seen on the water. He said, "It's about a size 17 blue-winged olive. You got any?" It was an answer I could believe. Since neither of us had any #17 Blue-Winged Olives, we went fishless until the hatch changed to the #18 we'd expected to find. It was a great example of size selectivity.

Carrying a small aquarium net in your vest at all times will help you find out the size and color of the naturals. I do it because I'm not always within earshot of my fishing partner. Besides, I want to see for myself exactly what the naturals look like.

At first glance the flavilinea appears to be nothing more than an immature green drake, but we should all know that an immature green drake is a nymph. The colors of the adult green drake and the flavilinea are very much the same; it's the size that can and does make a difference in catching success. I've been tying Green Drakes on Mustad's #12 94831 for years, and it's the perfect size match for the green drake. The flav is best imitated by using the same hook, but in #14. There are some proportional and minor color differences between the two flies as well, and I'm convinced that incorporating these differences can make your flav imitation more effective.

The Colorado green drake and the Henry's Fork green drake are almost identical in color and size. The big difference between the two is that the Henry's Fork fly has prominent yellow markings on both the body and the legs, while the Colorado version has no yellow; it's gray and green. On the other hand, I've found no color variations to the flav whether I'm in Colorado, Idaho, or Canada. The flav's tails are as long as the entire body, while the tails of the green drake are only half the body length, and the legs on the flav have brown and olive markings, as do the body segments.

Trout will often rise to a Flav when green drakes are hatching and it's still weeks before the flavs will begin. I have no idea what that's all about, but I thought it was worth mentioning. I'm to the point that I always carry a few Flavs with me no matter what's hatching. Here is my favorite Flavilinea recipe:

Hook:	Mustad 94831, #14.
Thread:	Danville's green monocord.
Tail:	Stiff brown spade hackle fibers.
Underbody:	Dub a short underbody with light green dubbing.
Overbody:	Green-dyed wild turkey biot.

Flavilinea Biot Dun

Wings: Pair of medium dun hen hackle tips.

Hackle: Brown and green-dyed grizzly.

1. Start the thread at midshank and tie in the spade hackle fiber tailing. Use about 25 percent more than you would on a standard #14 dry fly. The length should equal the entire hook.

2. Dub a #16 underbody, beginning one hook eye space ahead of the tailing. This space will allow the tie in of the biot tip in step 3. End the shoulder of the dubbed underbody about a hook-gap length behind the eye.

3. Tie in a green-dyed wild turkey biot by its tip (butt to the rear) just in front of the tailing with the fuzzy edge of the biot toward you with *only one turn* of thread.

4. Grasp the butt of the biot with your left thumb and forefinger and slide it away from you until it's at a 90-degree angle to the hook shank. Take three more very firm wraps of tying thread over the tip and the first turn of thread, and leave the bobbin hanging. This is the only way in which you can prevent a fold in the biot when you begin its first wrap around the hook.

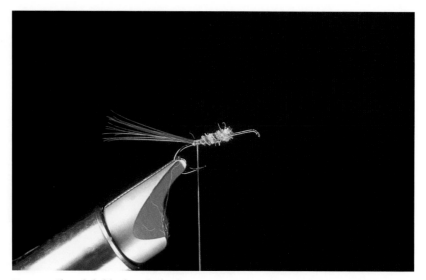

Dense tail and dubbed underbody

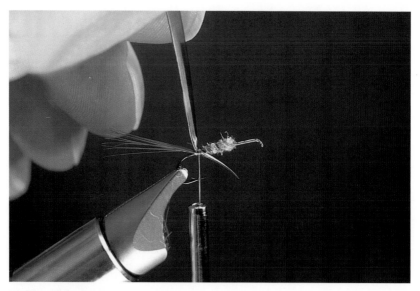

Biot at 90 degrees

5. Grasp the butt of the biot with your hackle pliers and make
    one turn around the hook shank. At the same time, follow the

biot with tying thread over the leading edge of the biot. This not only prevents the biot from slipping, but reinforces it as well.

Thread over leading edge of biot, half-done body

6. Continue in this manner until you reach the shoulder of the dubbed underbody. Take one or two turns of thread over the biot and clip off the butt.

7. Tie in a pair of medium dun hen hackle tip wings. The length should be equal to the entire hook.

8. Tie in a brown and a green grizzly hackle by their butts *in front of the wings*. Tips should be to the rear.

9. Begin wrapping with the brown hackle by pulling it straight away and down in front of the far wing. Bring the hackle underneath and complete the first turn of hackle *behind* the wings. Make two more turns of hackle behind the wings, then cross forward underneath the wing and continue wrapping hackle in front of the wings. Clip off the hackle butt.

Completed body with wings on and hackle tied in

10. Repeat step 9 with the green grizzly, clip off the tip, whip-finish, and apply a drop of head lacquer.

The flavilinea insect is a rather heavy bug that sits close to the surface. I like to clip the bottom hackle fibers even with the hook point to simulate the posture of the natural.

<u>PARACHUTE</u>

Sometimes trout will prefer a parachute mayfly imitation. The reasons for this are known only to the trout. I suspect it may be fishing pressure, or perhaps that a parachute resembles a sluggish dun. Whatever the reasons, it's important to carry a few parachute versions of all your mayfly patterns, especially the large drakes—which seem to interest bigger trout and more fly fishers. Here is my recipe for the Flavilinea Parachute.

Hook: Mustad 94831, #14.
Thread: Danville's green monocord.

Parachute Flavilinea

Tail:	Stiff brown spade hackle fibers.
Wing Post:	Segment of medium dun dyed white turkey T-base feather.
Underbody:	Dubbed short underbody with light green dubbing.
Overbody:	Green-dyed wild turkey biot.
Hackle:	One brown and one green-dyed grizzly.

1. Attach the thread one hook-gap space behind the eye and wrap to the beginning of the bend. Tie in a clump of stiff brown spade hackle fibers that's about 10 percent more than you used on the dun. The completed tail should be two hook-eye lengths longer than the entire hook. Lash the tailing butts forward to within half a hook-gap space behind the eye. Lift up the butts, clip them off, and cover the remaining hook shank with thread all the way to the eye. This provides a thread base upon which the wing post will be attached. Bring the thread back to the clipped tailing butts.

2. Select a large turkey T-base feather whose quill is centered. Clip out the quill from the tip of the feather to a distance equal to the

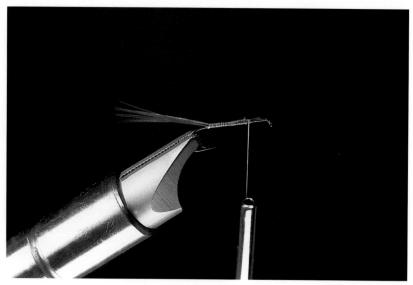

Tailing tied on

length of the entire hook. Pull all the marabou fibers away from the sides until each side is as wide as the hook shank is long, as shown in the upper photo on the facing page.

3. Fold the two halves together to form the wing post, place the post against the tyer's side of the hook at a 45-degree angle down (the tips should be forward), and tie it onto the hook immediately in front of the clipped tailing butts. Allow thread torque to push the post up on top of the hook. The wing post height should equal the hook-shank length. Take seven or eight very firm turns of thread.

4. Lift the butts, clip them off at a 45-degree angle, and cover the clipped butts with tying thread. Bring the thread forward to hang down immediately in front of the post.

5. Pull the wing post into an upright position, take nine or ten turns of thread in front of the post to form a thread dam to maintain a vertical position, apply a drop of head lacquer to the base of the post, and wrap the base with seven to ten turns of thread.

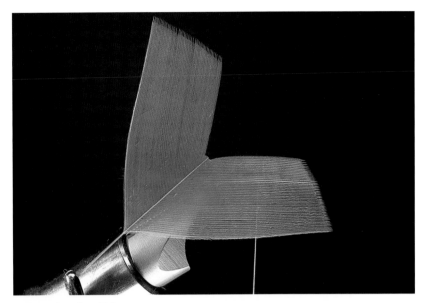

Prepared turkey T-base

Completed wing post

6. Apply dubbing as in the dun pattern to create a smooth carrot-shaped underbody all the way to the rear of the wing post.

7. Attach and wrap the biot overbody as in the dun pattern, but bring it forward under the wing post, tie it off in front of the post, and clip off the butt.

Completed body

8. Attach one brown and one green-dyed grizzly hackle feather. Take two turns of brown hackle and three turns of green grizzly hackle around the post. Clip off the hackle tips, whip-finish, and apply a drop of head lacquer.

FLAVILINEA SPINNER

I've had only about half a dozen opportunities to fish the flavilinea spinner fall and was damn glad I had a few imitations with me when it happened. On one such occasion there were some duns on the water and I could see a few large trout rising, but I couldn't so much as get a refusal rise after making thirty casts to the same fish. I looked into my fly box to decide what to try next when a flav spinner floated within inches of my knees. I tied on the spinner and took the trout of thirty casts on my next presentation.

Flavilinea Spinner

      Hook: Mustad 94831, #14.

   Thread: Danville's 429, tan monocord.

     Tail: Stiff light brown spade hackle fibers or Cocque de Leon tied splayed. The length should equal the entire hook plus two hook eyes.

Underbody: Tan dubbing.

Overbody: Dark tan dyed wild turkey biot.

  Wings: Pair of light medium dun dyed hen hackle tips.

Thorax: Dark tan dubbing.

Hackle: Dark tan dyed grizzly.

1. Start the thread on the hook half a hook-gap space behind the eye and wrap to the beginning of the bend. Create a little thread

bump over the last wrap of thread to splay the tailing. Tie on a sparse clump of stiff hackle fibers and splay the tips by pushing down on the fibers immediately in front of the thread bump. Apply a tiny drop of head lacquer to the base of the tails. Lash the butts down to within half a hook-gap space of the hook eye.

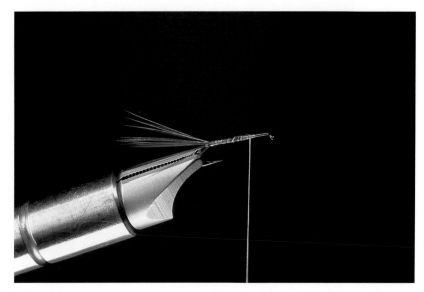

Splayed tailing

2. Bring the tying thread back toward the bend of the hook and dub a thinly tapered underbody to the end of the clipped tailing butts. Bring the tying thread back to the beginning of the bend.

3. Attach the turkey biot and wind it forward as described in Chapter fourteen, "Indestructible Biots," tie off in front of the shoulder of the underbody, and clip off the butt.

4. Tie in a pair of heavily webbed hen hackle tips whose width is equal to the hook-gap space and whose length is equal to the entire hook. Figure-eight wrap between the wings with tying thread to separate and flatten them to a horizontal position.

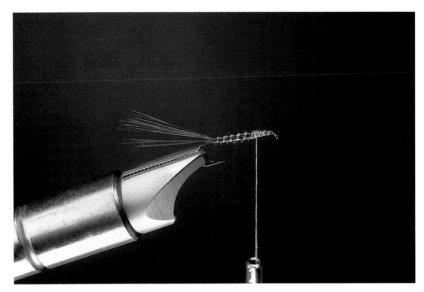

Completed body

Wings in position

5. Tie in the brown grizzly by its butt behind the wings and on top of the hook with the dull side up.

6. Loosely dub and figure-eight a slightly fat thorax around and between the wings.

Thorax with hackle tied in

7. Wind the hackle forward in four slightly open turns. Take two spaced turns behind the wings, cross forward beneath the wings, and take two more spaced turns in front of the wings. Use enough tension on the hackle to bury the stem in the soft thorax. Tie off the tip, snip away the excess, whip-finish, and apply a drop of head lacquer to the head.

8. Clip all the hackle fibers away from the bottom of the fly.

SIXTEEN

Lime Trude

—————————————— ✳

"Papa, there's no hatch. What fly should we use?" asked Nick, my fifteen-year-old grandson. I've been giving him advice (fly fishing only) since he was ten years old on our first annual camping/trout-fishing excursion on the St. Vrain River in Colorado. Nick's an excellent fly fisher for a fifteen-year-old. Roughly translated, his question was "How are we going to catch breakfast?"

Only a year before, John Gierach and I were fishing near Fernie, British Columbia, with guide Dave Brown under the same conditions. Dave said, "Here, try a Lime Trude, eh?" There was no hatch for hours that day, but we all wore out a couple of Lime Trudes as native cutthroat trout gobbled them on what seemed like every fourth or fifth cast.

That day in B.C. flashed through my mind as I looked through my box of Royal Wulffs and Adams. In one corner there were three #14 Lime Trudes. I handed one to Nick and said, "Here, try a Lime Trude, eh?" Two 12-inch rainbows and a couple of 10-inch brookies went into the frying pan about 10:30 A.M. The Lime Trudes had been so productive that it was hard for us to quit fishing just to eat!

The Lime Trude is one of those attractor patterns that will often produce when there's no hatch, or when none of the usual "flies of last resort" work. My theory is that every trout in the country has already seen hundreds of Royal Wulffs and Adams. The Lime Trude looks enough like some kind of insect that trout will strike the fly out of what I like to think is an inborn predatory instinct, and the white calf tail wing makes them very easy for fly fishers to see.

Lime Trude

Tying the Lime Trude (or any other color, for that matter) doesn't require any special advanced tying skill. But there are a few little tricks that I employ to make this fly behave the way I want.

  Hook: Your favorite dry-fly hook, #10 through 16.
Thread: Black 6/0.
  Tail: Well-marked golden pheasant tippets.

Body: Lime green fine dry-fly dubbing.

Wing: White calf tail.

Hackle: Lots of stiff brown saddle.

1. Start the thread on the hook about half a hook-gap distance behind the eye and cover the shank with thread all the way to the hook bend. I normally don't start my thread this close to the hook eye, but in the case of the Lime Trude, I'll be tying in a rather full hairwing and I want it to be easily locked in place.

2. Tie in a segment of well-marked golden pheasant tippets to be about hook-gap length. Select a feather that will display the black–gold–black markings. Clip out a segment of fibers about half as wide as the hook gap, and roll them to keep the vibrant colors to the outside of the clump.

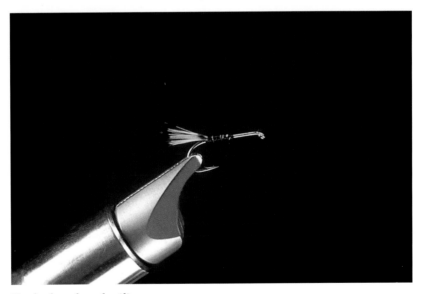

Hook, thread, and tailing

3. Use the finest dry-fly dubbing you can find for the body. Blend it to a light chartreuse color, keeping in mind that most dubbing will darken when you apply a floatant. Dub the body material

onto the thread as tightly as you can and create a full reverse taper to the body, stopping a full hook-gap space behind the eye of the hook.

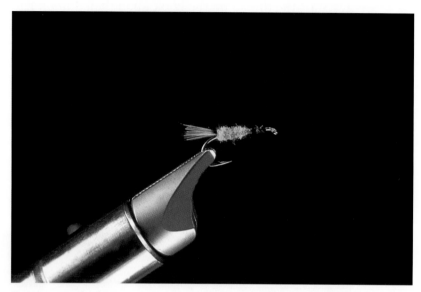

Reverse taper body

4. Use the straightest white calf tail you have. Remove all the short hair, stack it well, and create a rather full downwing to extend slightly beyond the tip of the tail. Clip off the wing butts at an angle slightly behind the eye of the hook, leaving about half a hook-eye space of bare hook shank behind the eye for the head and whip-finish. Apply a drop of thin head lacquer and completely cover all the white hair butts with tying thread.

5. Using the stiffest brown hackle you can find (I prefer top-quality saddle on this fly), wrap a very dense hackle collar with as many turns of hackle as you can without crowding the hook eye.

I use just about every kind of trick imaginable when I fish this fly. I dead-drift it, smack it into the water with an overpowered cast, bounce it off overhanging leaves, twitch it, skate it, hand-retrieve it, and yank it beneath the surface for a few seconds of wet-fly use. I

Wing

also like to skip it upstream when I'm fishing riffle water. All of this is asking a lot from a single fly, but it can be done if you'll tie yours as described above.

Nick and I were back on the stream at about 2:00 P.M. and found a good hatch of Red Quills, but we stayed with the Lime Trudes and caught far more than our share of trout, quitting in time to find our way back to the campsite for a fireside dinner of Dinty Moore Stew. As we zipped up our sleeping bags much later that evening, Nick asked, "Do you think I should fish that Lime Trude again tomorrow?"

"You bet!" I said, "but we should probably find some new water."

SEVENTEEN

Sparkle Wing Caddis

✳

I'm constantly looking for ways to improve the effectiveness of my favorite patterns. Some days I seem to spend more time watching insects and the trout that feed on them than I do fishing. I occasionally discover something I didn't know, such as a little sparkle in the wings of most airborne caddisflies, especially during sunset hours, when most caddis hatches I have observed seem to occur.

The addition of a sparse underwing of light dun mink tail guard hair on your fluttering caddis will make a very effective fly. The key word here is *sparse,* for both the mink tail guard hair and the elk- or deer-hair overwing. Caddisfly wings are translucent to some degree at rest, and especially so when they're fluttering in an attempt to get airborne. A good way to determine if you have the correct amount of winging material on your caddisfly is to look at it from the top. If you can see the body of the fly through the wing, you've got it right. Most hairwing caddis patterns are tied with enough hair in the wing to tie two or three flies. A sparse mink tail guard hair underwing and the sparkle it adds makes this pattern much better than the original.

Sparkle Wing Caddis

SPARKLE WING CADDIS

Hook: Your favorite dry-fly hook, #14 through 20.

Thread: Yellow, prewaxed 6/0 or 8/0.

Body: Very fine pale yellow dry-fly dubbing; I prefer rabbit belly underfur.

Underwing: Sparse light dun mink tail guard hair.

Overwing: Sparse light ginger elk or deer body hair (no black tips); bleached is adequate, but be careful that the bleaching process didn't make the hair brittle.

Hackle: Ginger to match overwing color.

1. Start the tying thread on the hook above the hook point and wrap to the beginning of the bend.

2. Apply very small amounts of dubbing to the thread to create a very clean reverse taper to a point one third of a hook-shank length behind the eye of the hook. The body should taper to hook-shank diameter at the point of winging. This is to prevent

flaring the wing more than you should. Leave the thread hanging at the front end of the body.

3. Clip a small bundle of mink tail hair, remove the underfur, stack it to even the tips, and place the bundle on top of the hook shank with the tips extending beyond the end of the hook bend by the distance of one hook gap. The diameter of the bundle should be slightly less than half the diameter of a round toothpick, and slightly less for smaller flies.

4. Tie the bundle in with very secure thread wraps and manipulate the hair to come around to the halfway point on either side of the hook. Clip the hair butts to reveal enough space for the hackle tie-off and head, and apply a drop of head cement to the thread wraps over the mink hair. Return the thread to the beginning of the body.

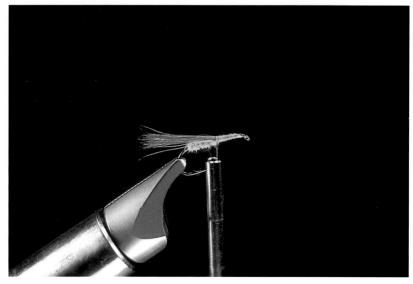

Mink tail underwing tied in and distributed, and butts clipped

5. Clip a small bundle of elk or deer body hair, remove the underfur, stack it to even the tips, and apply it to the hook just as you

did with the mink tail guard hair underwing. Be sure to distribute the hair evenly on each side of the hook. The diameter of this bundle should be about the same diameter as a round toothpick, slightly less for smaller flies. Allow the tips of the overwing to extend beyond the underwing by a distance of one hook eye. Bind to the hook very firmly, lift the butts, and clip to reveal enough space for the hackle tie-off and head. Apply head cement to the hairwing tie-in. Return the thread to the beginning of the body.

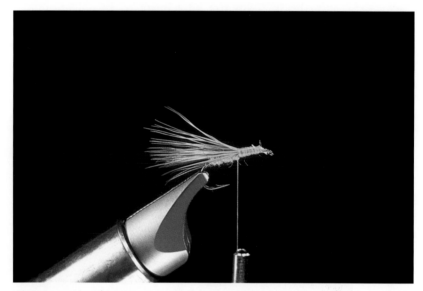

Elk hair tied in, distributed, and butts clipped

Note: It's important to evenly distribute both the mink tail guard hair and the elk hair to each side of the hook to simulate the rear pair of legs of the natural, which always extend to the end of the wing. This will also provide some stability to your fly.

6. Select your very best dry-fly hackle, and create a hackle collar that takes up the front third of the hook.

7. Whip-finish and apply head lacquer.

This pattern is one of few in which I apply head lacquer while tying. The mink tail guard hair is very hard and slippery, and will tend to twist when you tie on the overwing. You must tie this fly with a thread tension that is near the breaking point and add head lacquer as well, both of which will ensure a durable fly.

EIGHTEEN

Clumsy Caddis

＊

Caddisflies can be just as clumsy as mayflies. Everything about their well-known "pop out" emergence doesn't always work perfectly. A significant number of emerging caddis will injure one wing, which can adhere to the surface film and cause quite a commotion while the adult tries its very best to get airborne before it becomes lunch for a hungry trout. Once again, trout get them all and you'll never see them unless you're lying on your belly looking straight down on a feeding lane. You can learn a lot if you lie still as a log with your nose 12 to 20 inches above the stream.

CLUMSY CADDIS

Hook:	Your favorite dry-fly hook, size to match the naturals.
Thread:	Match body color.
Body:	Fine dry-fly dubbing. Create a reverse taper to the body of all caddis patterns.

Caddis, top view

Caddis, front view

Downwing: Hen hackle tip, tied to lie horizontal and flat on the water.

Hairwing: Sparse elk or deer body hair only slightly flared.

Hackle: Extra-select dry-fly hackle, color appropriate to the natural.

1. Dub a reverse-tapered body as in step 2 for the Sparkle Wing Caddis. A reverse taper allows you to tie in the hairwing without causing excess flaring of the elk- or deer-hair wing that will be added later.

2. Tie in one slender hen hackle tip on the far side of the hook immediately in front of the thin body. It's easier to control the placement of the wing for right-handed tyers by placing the wing on the far side of the hook. Clip the feather to length, but do not trim the hackle fibers from the base of the hackle tip before tying it in. The soft hackle fibers will help prevent the wing from twisting as you wrap thread around it. Be certain that its tip extends beyond the end of the hook bend by one hook-gap distance and that it will lie flat on the water, as shown in the photo below.

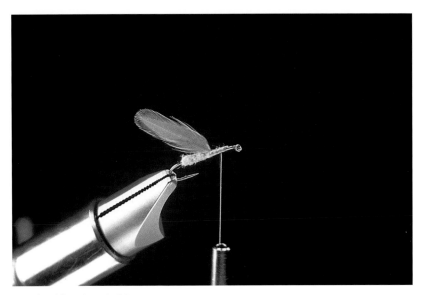

Hen hackle wing tied in

3. Clip a small clump of elk or deer body hair, remove all the underfur, and stack it in a hair stacker. The diameter of the amount of hair you should apply to the hook should be no larger than the diameter of a standard wooden kitchen match. Keep it sparse!

4. Lash the bundle of body hair to the top of the hook, being very careful not to destroy the position of the hen hackle tip downwing. Hair tips should extend beyond the bend by one hook-gap space and be evenly distributed on each side of the hook.

5. Tie in the hackle and wind forward as usual.

Hair bundle tied in and clipped

Note: It's often a good idea to clip all the hackle flush with the bottom of the body of the Clumsy Caddis, which will make it appear even more vulnerable to the trout. Substitute body, wing, and hackle colors to imitate other caddis species.

Keep the following thought in mind: Mother Nature provides many imperfections in her perfect system. The imperfections will always be food for the predators. It's what makes the system work so perfectly.

Of course, this discussion involves a certain degree of theory, but most of fly fishing is based on theories. My latest is to never go fishing without my trusty fly box full of Clumsy Caddis. It's always a good idea to give any caddis pattern an occasional tiny twitch to imitate the struggling natural. Keep your rod tip within an inch of the surface at a 90-degree angle to your fly line—and be ready!

NINETEEN

Large Caddis

—————————————————— ✳ ————

Anyone who fly fishes should carry a few #6 or 8 caddis from spring to late fall. Many streams and lakes in North America have hatches of these large insects, which are often overlooked by the casual visitor or mistaken for stoneflies. The hatch is usually sparse, and brings only a few trout to the surface, but these fish are often the biggest in the water. I caught one of the biggest brown trout of my life in an Alberta beaver pond on a #6 Olive Hairwing Caddis. The 23-inch fish sucked it down with all the confidence of a largemouth bass! A lucky cast beneath an overhanging spruce branch on an otherwise fishless day convinced me to carry a few Large Caddis no matter where I go fishing during the normal dry-fly season. I've found hatches of giant yellow caddis in some of the alpine lakes in Colorado, huge brown caddis in Labrador, and big olive caddis in Alberta. Luckily I had a few Large Caddis tucked away in each of the above situations, and they saved the day for me.

Large Caddis often must be presented with long casts in nearly impossible-to-reach places. My fly takes a hell of a beating as I try to retrieve it from the bushes behind me or yank it loose from the branches on the other side of the stream. As a result, these large flies must be very durable and highly buoyant. Tying these bugs so they are durable, float high, and can be twitched or skittered without drowning takes a little time, but it's well worth the effort. A crucial component is the use of monocord. Forget about the 8/0 and 14/0 tying threads used on little flies.

#6 Olive Caddis

LARGE CADDIS

Hook:	Mustad 94831 or Tiemco 5262, #6 through 10.
Thread:	Monocord to match body dubbing color.
Underbody:	Hollow elk hair, hook-shank length.
Overbody:	Fine dry-fly dubbing to within one hook-gap space of hook eye.
Wing:	Brown elk with light tips for Brown and Olive Caddis, blond elk for Yellow Caddis.

> *Hackle:* The stiffest hackle you can find, and plenty of it! Fifteen to seventeen wraps of hackle is about right. Use brown hackle for Olive and Brown Caddis, and Light Ginger Hackle for Yellow Caddis.

1. Cover the entire hook with monocord beginning one hook-eye space behind the eye and continuing to the beginning of the hook bend. Bring the thread back to within two hook-eye spaces of the hook eye.

2. Clip a small clump of elk hair (about the diameter of a wooden kitchen match), remove the underfur, stack the tips, and clip off the butts at a point where they are all even.

3. Place the elk bundle on top of the hook with the tips pointing forward over the hook eye by a distance of about 1 inch. Lash the bundle to the top of the hook in open wraps of thread (about one-eighth inch spacing) to within one hook-eye space of the bend. Take three or four turns of thread, lift the elk butts, and clip them off at an angle. Cross-wrap the thread back to the initial tie-down, clip off the excess tips, and cover the clipped tips with two or three turns of tying thread. Cross-wrap the thread back to the bend and cover the clipped butts with thread. Tying the thicker hair butts to the rear of the hook will help create reverse taper to the body as well as add some flotation.

4. Firmly twist dubbing onto the thread and carefully wrap the dubbing forward to avoid any spaces in the dubbing wraps. Stop the dubbing at a point one hook-gap space behind the eye, and firmly lay a base of thread over the elk tips to the hook eye and back to the shoulder of the body.

5. Clip a clump of elk about three-sixteenths inch in diameter, remove the underfur, and stack the tips in a stacker.

6. Align the hair tips to extend beyond the hook bend by a distance equal to one hook gap, and tie the bundle to the top of the hook immediately in front of the shoulder of the body. Wrap tying thread with increasing tension over the butts to within one hook-eye space of the eye. Lift the butts, clip them off at an

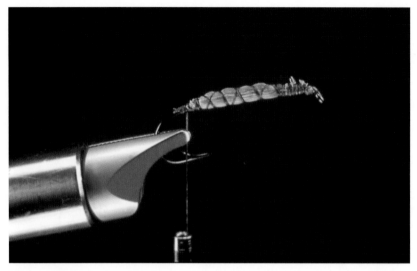

Elk underbody

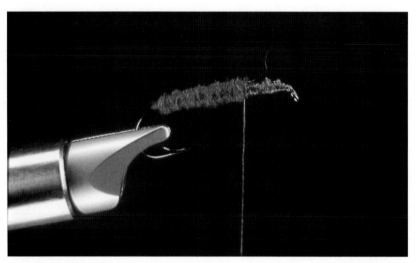

Dubbing overbody

angle, and cover the clipped ends with a couple of wraps of thread. Bring the thread back to the shoulder area.

Elk wing tied in

7. Select two or three of the stiffest hackles you can find and clip away all the webbing from near the base of each feather. Tie the hackles in immediately in front of the shoulder of the body and wrap forward to within one hook-eye space of the eye. Tie off, trim the hackle tips, whip-finish with at least seven turns, and apply a liberal drop of head lacquer.

The Large Caddis and the Woolly Bugger are two trout flies that I make every attempt to tie as bulletproof as possible.

TWENTY

Butt Faced Lemmings

---- ✳

John Gierach and I have made three trips to Ann Marie Lodge in Labrador for the giant brook trout that Lee Wulff discovered there about forty years ago. Careful management of this fabulous resource has ensured the quantity and size of these marvelous fish. Lodge brochures advertise that the *average* Ann Marie Lake brook trout is in excess of 5 pounds, and I can vouch for the fact that this is true. Guides begin recording daily catches of trout of 2 pounds and up, but there seems to be more 3- to 6½-pounders than there are 2-pounders. Brook trout from 2 to 7 pounds happily rise to dry flies. Depending on the time of year, the flies could be #16 Blue Quills, #18 Pale Tan Skittering Caddis, #12 Green Drakes, or, if all else fails, #10 Royal Wulff. Several 8-pounders are landed each year. I had a little trouble that first year believing that a 1½-pound brook trout didn't count.

Our second trip to the lodge was a little different in that one of the guides called to advise us to bring plenty of mouse flies. The

"Lemming?"

lemming migration would be taking place while we were going to be there. Neither of us had the time to tie up a dozen or more deer-hair mice, so (it hurts to admit this) we both ordered a couple dozen of those cute little deer-hair mice that you'll see in fly shops all over the country. They really are cute, with their shiny little beady eyes and just the right number of whiskers, pointy little noses, and round ears in just the right place. Even the tails are nice and soft.

The trouble was that lemmings are more than twice the size of any mouse fly, and they swim as fast as we could execute a hand retrieve. When we tried that with our little pointy-nose-mouse patterns, they dove beneath the surface. No amount of trimming or field dressing could solve the problem. Brook trout and huge pike were inhaling live lemmings all over the lake and we caught only one or two fish on our mouse patterns the first time we tried them.

That night, I visited the guide's shack and asked Randy, the head guide, if he had a big brown bucktail and some stinger hooks. He handed me a partially used medium-sized bucktail and a box of #4 streamer hooks. There was only enough brown hair remaining on the bucktail to tie four flies. I gave two to John and kept two for myself. They were a little crude, but the results the next day were fantastic. Below is my recipe for what I called the "Butt Faced Lemming."

Now this *is a Lemming!*

Hook: Daiichi 2461, #4/0 (or any #4/0 4X-long freshwater streamer hook).

Thread: Danville's monocord, 100, black.

Tail: Brown bucktail.

Body: Brown bucktail.

Head: Brown bucktail (hollow hair from the base of the tail).

1. Attach tying thread near the bend of the hook and wrap forward for only about one-quarter inch. Bring the thread back to the beginning of the bend and apply a drop of head lacquer.

Tail:

2. Select a one-quarter-inch-diameter clump of brown bucktail at least 2 inches long and clip it from the skin as close as you can. Remove all the underfur and shorter hair.

3. Use the pinch-and-pull method to even the tips a little. Don't make them all the same length.

4. Tie the clump onto the hook over the starting thread wraps and allow the hair to roll evenly around the hook. Take several firm wraps of thread for a distance of about one-quarter inch and apply a drop of head lacquer.

5. Lift the hair butts and trim as close to the thread wraps as possible, creating an abrupt shoulder. The first clump of bucktail should appear as in the photo below.

Tail clump tied in

Body:

6. Select another larger clump of hair (about ½ inch in diameter) and repeat the process in steps 2, 3, 4, and 5. However, when placing the clump on the hook, be sure that the hair tips will be at least 1 inch shorter than the tail clump.

7. Tie the second clump immediately in front of the butts of the first clump and allow the bucktail to roll completely around the hook. Apply enough thread pressure to cause the hair to flare slightly, as in the photo on page 215.

Second hair clump

8. Repeat with a third clump as in steps 6 and 7. Be sure that it's the same length as the second clump before it was tied in. The tips of each of the body clumps should be one-quarter inch shorter than the previous clump.

9. Continue adding clumps until you're within one-half inch of the hook eye. Put a drop of head lacquer over each tie-down.

Head:

10. Select a clump of hollow hair from the base of the deer tail. Clip it off, remove the underfur, and clip the hair tips so that you have a clump of hollow hair about 1 inch long. Spin it as you would when tying a bass bug and pack it firmly.

11. Continue spinning and packing the head until there's just enough space remaining for the thread head. Whip-finish and apply a drop of head lacquer.

12. Trim the flared head to a round shape that is even with the hook point.

Third hair clump

Body complete

13.   Apply a generous amount of thick head lacquer to the face of the fly to keep it flat. Alternatively, if you don't lacquer the face, the hair will bend back slightly while you cast and retrieve to present a little less wind and water resistance.

The beauty of this fly is that it floats heavily in the water like a live lemming, but it doesn't sink, and it's almost weedless. When you cast it into a patch of lily pads, the broad flat face makes the rear of the fly swing around to the side, which usually prevents snags on the stems. This action also makes it irresistible to trout and pike. When hand-retrieved at a steady pace, the fly will create a wake much like a live lemming. If you use a jerky hand retrieve, the fly will resemble a lemming that is tiring. The Butt Faced Lemming has some air resistance when cast. I recommend at least a WF7F line and a 3X leader tippet. The strikes can be vicious. Keep your rod tip at an angle to the fly line so that the tip can absorb some of the shock. I've had large fish snap 3X as though it were 7X simply because I had my rod tip pointed directly at the fly. Now I keep my rod at a 90-degree angle to my fly line and the rod tip within an inch or two of the water's surface, which prevents any slack in the fly line when I strike back.

I know the Butt Faced Lemming works for large brook trout and pike in Labrador. I'd be willing to bet a six-pack or two that it'll work just as well when cast over large brown trout and bass on a quiet evening.

TWENTY-ONE

Field Dressing Flies and the Fly-Tying Travel Kit

✳

I'm not one to have many gadgets hanging on the front of my vest, but the one tool I wouldn't be without is a small pair of expensive fly-tying scissors that I keep on a strong zinger. They have short, fine blades that are slightly serrated. I like them a lot better than those little gadgets that look like part of a pair of fingernail clippers, because I don't have to thread tippet or leader material into a narrow one-eighth-inch slot. I can also trim the hackle from the bottom of any size of dry fly closer and cleaner to the thorax area with scissors. I can even trim a broken fingernail, or clip off the grass seed stem that snagged my sloppy backcast. It works on small willow branches, too.

It's almost impossible to carry flies whose tails, wings, and hackles are always exactly the correct length or density for every specific condition. This is especially true if you have to purchase some flies when you're out on a day trip. In these instances, we need to fine-tune some flies a little to make them more effective. I call it field dressing. I can field dress nearly any fly with these little fly-tying scissors. For example:

1. Dry-fly tail too dense? Use the very tips of the fine pointed scissors to clip away some of the top tailing fibers. I usually try to clip out some of the center fibers as well to give the fly a split-tail appearance.

2. Dry-fly wings too tall? It's an easy matter to pinch them together between your thumb and forefinger and trim to a new length while shaping them as well.

3. Biot nymph tails too long? Once again it's a simple job to clip them at angle, which will shorten and reshape them.

4. Caddis dry-fly hairwing too bushy? Use the fine points to clip away some of the hair from the top of the wing where it's tied in.

5. Need to create a Clumsy Dun? Twist the wings and hackle collar to one side and clip all the hackle from the bottom of the fly. This will put one wing on the water and simulate a clumsy fly that fell over or got blown over.

6. Is the hairwing on your streamer too long? Use the fine points to clip out the hair in different lengths from the end of the wing and gradually shorten the entire wing. Never clip it off abruptly.

7. Feather-wing streamer wings too long? Hold the wing tips together between your thumb and forefinger and shorten and shape them at the same time. Use the end of your thumb as a guide; it's almost the perfect curve.

8. Do you want a fuzzier body on a nymph? Close the points of your scissors and pick out the body just as you would with a bodkin. Use the point of one blade to pick out the bodies on small nymphs.

9. Did a trout's tooth snag some peacock herl and leave tag ends trailing from the body of your fly? Clip them flush with the body with the fine points of your scissors.

10. Ribbing wire or floss rib come loose? Clip it off. Never try to pull it, or you may destroy the entire fly.

11. Hackle collar not bushy enough? Close the scissor points and burnish the hackle stem wraps with the outside edge of the

blades. This will often flatten the hackle quills sufficiently to make the hackle fibers bush forward and back just enough to make the fly a little more effective by distributing its contact points along the surface.

12. If the antenna fibers that were tied on your fly aren't needed, don't pull them off, because you may destroy the head. Clip them off.

13. Need an emerger when all you have are dry flies? Give a ratty old dry fly a haircut. Snip away at it until it begins to look like an emerger: stubby tail, short hackle, and just a little wing.

14. Need to make a spinner from a dry-fly dun? Clip all the hackle from the bottom of the fly, press the wings out horizontally, and tie a figure-eight knot through them with a length of 7X or 8X tippet. It may not be pretty, but it works.

15. Yarn strike indicator too big? Clip some of it off with your scissors.

16. Threads caught in the zippers of your vest? Don't pull them out—they may be the very threads that hold the zipper to the pocket. Cut them away with your scissors.

Don't let yourself get locked into the thought that you don't have the right fly and so you're not going to catch any fish. You will always have at least one fly in one of your fly boxes that you can field dress into what might just be a new killer pattern!

Streamside tying is something I've never done well. It takes too much time from my fishing; also, my hands begin to quiver as I attempt to tie a new pattern or pattern alteration while listening to trout rising a short cast away. There always seems to be just enough breeze to whisk away the one piece of material I desperately need to finish the fly, and the addition of more tools and materials to my already heavy vest is more than I care to deal with.

Longer trips are a different matter. I can't remember how many times I've been out on a weeklong trip only to find an unexpected hatch—and I didn't have the right fly, or the local fly shop didn't have any matching flies in stock. Once I lost a fly box that contained the only flies that would have solved the problem. That's why I've learned to always take along a fly-tying travel kit for seven- to ten-day trips to far-off destinations where the advance information was written by someone who was more interested in the gourmet food and fine wines at the lodge than in local hatches.

When I drive my truck on a fishing trip that's going to last a week or longer, I always pack a large tying kit that contains everything I could possibly need—and a lot that I'll probably never need. Sometimes it's fun to sit around camp and tie a few flies when there's no hatch on. It's about the only time I have to fill out my fly boxes. However, if I'm going to fly to some distant location, I'm faced with space and weight constrictions. I refuse to take more bags than I can carry in one trip. That usually means a day pack, a rod tube, and a duffel. My shaving kit, reels, fly boxes, camera, film, rain shell, and a canteen of water usually fill the day pack. That leaves the rod tube with two or three rods, and the duffel for clothes, waders, vest, hat, net, and a small space for a fly-tying kit. So once again, I'm faced with some agonizing choices on what fly-tying materials I think I will *really* need.

Over the years I have pared down the amount of fly-tying stuff I pack for air travel to what I call my Fly-Tying Survival Kit. The materials in it will allow me to tie most of the common nymphs, dry flies, and streamers, or be able to get close enough to the natural that it really doesn't matter.

Here's my Survival Kit. All of it will fit into one large 12½-by-18-inch padded mailing envelope, which I can usually squeeze into a space between my wading boots and waders.

HOOKS

Dry fly in #12 through 26; streamer in #4 through 12; twelve of each. Get several seven-day "pill minders" at your local drugstore. They make great containers for small numbers of hooks.

TOOLS

Vise, bobbin cradle, materials holder, two scissors, bobbin, hackle pliers, hair stacker, bodkin, dubbing teaser, and bobbin threader.

Never pack head lacquer for air travel. Chances are that air-pressure changes will cause it to leak and ruin all your materials.

THREADS

6/0: black, white, olive, yellow, and tan. Single-strand red floss and monocord in black and yellow.

BRASS BEADING WIRE

28 gauge and 32 gauge, one spool each.

LEAD WIRE SUBSTITUTE

.030-inch diameter, 30 inches.

DUBBING

Rabbit: black, white, olive, tan, brown, yellow, gray (all guard hairs removed). Blended hare's mask in natural and olive colors. Pack each color in a labeled empty hook box.

STRIPPED AND DYED ROOSTER NECK HACKLE QUILLS

Olive, tan, gray, cream, yellow, black, brown (two dozen each)

NECKS DRY-FLY HALF NECKS

Grizzly, brown, medium dun, medium ginger, black, cream/white. Or pull a dozen hackles of each size and put them in labeled plastic Ziploc sleeves. This could save a lot of space—but don't forget to pull some tailing material as well. Also, medium dun and white hen necks, and a mottled brown hen back or neck.

TURKEY T-BASE

White and dyed dun (twelve each)

POLY YARN

Gray and white (1 foot each)

CHENILLE

Medium sized, olive and black (2 feet of each)

YARN

Yellow, olive, and black (2 feet of each)

SPARKLE BRAID

Gold, silver, pearl (2 feet each)

KRYSTAL FLASH

Pearlescent

MARABOU

Black, white, olive (twelve each)

GRAY AND FOX SQUIRREL TAILS (TOP HALF OF EACH)

BUCKTAILS

One-half natural bucktail with medium to dark brown center. Small pieces of yellow-, red-, and green-dyed bucktail

WHITE TAIL DEER BODY HAIR STRIPS

Light and dark, one-half inch wide by 3 inches long

ELK-HAIR STRIPS

Light and dark one-half inch wide by 3 inches long

MOOSE BODY HAIR STRIP

One-half inch wide by 3 inches long

PAIR OF WILD TURKEY SECONDARY WING QUILLS, SPRAYED WITH KRYLON

PAIR OF DARK GOOSE SECONDARY WING QUILLS, SPRAYED WITH KRYLON

PAIR OF WILD TURKEY CENTER TAIL FEATHERS WITH PROMINENT BLACK BAR, SPRAYED WITH KRYLON

PAIR OF RING-NECKED PHEASANT TAIL CENTER QUILLS

Pack only enough of any material to tie a dozen flies of any kind. This will keep down the bulk when you're packing for a flight to Timbuktu. You'd be wise to check with customs regulations both into and out of a foreign country so that you don't have all your natural materials confiscated at the border!

Index

✳